$\mathcal{W}$HY
IS IT SO HARD
TO TAKE CARE OF
MY PARENT?

BY

LINDA MEYER, PH.D.

Recovery Communications, Inc.
P.O. Box 19910, Baltimore, Maryland 21211 • (410) 243-8558

To receive our free monthly e-mail newsletter, please visit our website at
http://www.RecoveryCommunications.com

Excerpts from Loretta Starr's essay "Walking With Uncle Bill," written in conjunction with her participation in Shalem Institute's Spiritual Guidance Program, appeared in the September 1998 issue of *Shalem News*. An edited version is reprinted here by permission of Shalem Institute for Spiritual Formation, 5430 Grosvenor Lane, Bethesda, MD 20814, and the author. "Walking With Uncle Bill" © copyright 1998 by Loretta Starr.

ISBN 1-891874-05-5

To

My parents, Louise and Winfield Meyer —
your spirits are always with me

My brother, Fred, who supported me
every inch of the way in caring for our mother

My husband, Don, who "just knew" and
was always here when I needed him

Our closest friends, who listened to us
with great patience and spelled us when asked

The numerous caregivers who lovingly cared for
my mother, especially Ellen and Bobbie
who were with us through the end

TABLE OF CONTENTS

INTRODUCTION

If you have picked up this book, chances are you are already facing the issues of eldercare. More and more Americans must do so as baby-boomers reach middle age, the general population gets older, and people live longer.

As a therapist and mediator who works with individuals and families, I have compiled these stories and suggestions both from my counseling experience and as someone who has dealt successfully with eldercare issues in my own family. In spite of the challenges — some major ones — I shall value the rewards I gained through caring for my elderly mother as long as I live. I hope that your own experience can be an equally rewarding one.

Eldercare issues sneak up on us. Suddenly one day we are in the eldercare soup whether we want to be or not, and regardless of whether we have made plans to cope with the situation if it were to arise.

When families have a new baby, or are expecting one, the world beats a path to their door with congratulations, gift showers, greeting cards, and invitations for everything from a subscription to a childcare magazine, to a Money Market account for the little stranger.

Yet when we undertake the care of an elderly relative or friend, nothing like that happens. Our friends seem sympathetic, but a celebration of Grannie's entry into the household is unheard of. No department store has an Old Folks' department, although Babies' and Children's departments abound. No magazines offer to help us with our day-to-day eldercare concerns. No one ever presents Uncle Joe with a fancy gift-wrapped nightshirt. And no mental-health professional or minister hangs out a sign advertising "What To Do When Gramps or Grannie Comes To Your House To Live." The truth is, families are rarely knowledgeable or joyful about any eldercare situation they may face. Most of us assume the only thing to do is grit our teeth and soldier on.

The message of this book is much more positive. It is intended as a companion for anyone undertaking to care for an elderly relative or friend, or just beginning to consider the issues. Eldercare, like childcare, is a normal stage of life. Hundreds of thousands of adult children have faced these issues, lived to tell about them, and been grateful for the experience. Many of us have taken pride in handling our challenges and found grace and humor in what might have been horribly dreary situations. Elderly family members by the thousands are able to say that their relatives, or friends, care for them diligently and extremely well.

This book's core reality is this: Alone, I can do very little. But with the help of a good support network and a Higher Power, any one of us can care for our elders with happiness and success.

— Linda Meyer
Champaign, Illinois

Why Is It So Hard To Take Care Of My Parent?

Is It Time To Order Bifocals?

This is a question for you — not your parents. All of us age, some more gracefully than others. How are you dealing with your own aging process? Why is this question important?

We have ample evidence today that young and middle-aged Americans are having a great deal of difficulty with aging. Some baby-boomers appear to believe that they will be able to stave off the aging process indefinitely. Many of us view our parents as having always been old, while believing that we ourselves can somehow remain forever young. Wishful thinking!

Dealing with parents' aging is often closely tied to our own thoughts and feelings about growing old. Those of us who see aging as a process that everyone will go through usually handle the inevitable changes in our parents more easily than others do.

This is where bifocals come in. If you are already wearing them, you can skip the remainder of this paragraph. If not, how many times have you tripped going up or down stairs? Are you no longer able to read the paper without glasses? If so, what have you done about it? Are you still buying your glasses at the drugstore, if it is legal in your state, or do you have to switch glasses every few minutes as your activities change?

Bifocals are a useful adjunct to midlife. They are also a symbol of one's own aging process. Can you accept their usefulness along with the message they are sending about aging in your life?

"The Insurance Company Called. Your Dad's Had Another Fender-Bender."

The most classic example of the struggle older folk put up to remain independent centers around driving a car. Most of us who have ever driven, and who live anywhere other than a large city, hang on to our privilege of driving like grim death — often past the point that we can safely do so.

Talk with a teenager about their visits with grandparents, and one of the first things you are likely to hear is how poorly their grandparents drive. Christie, age 20, and her 23-year-old brother Brett visited their octogenarian grandmother and came home with many tales of the curbs Grandma was regularly climbing as she drove. Yet Grandma and her 85-year-old sister both still drive the California freeways.

My mother was quite the opposite. When she moved to our town to be near me — a plan we had agreed would be desirable — she drove her car 90 miles, parked it in front of my house, and never drove again. Perhaps the difference was that she had been talking consistently of moving here so that I could help look after her, or perhaps she just didn't want to undertake driving in a new town. Maybe she even recognized the toll that her drinking was taking (unlikely). But once she stopped driving, the burden of her transportation needs fell squarely on me.

Bob's 77-year-old widowed father, John, still lived alone. He had been dreading seeing his ophthalmologist for fear of being told he must give up driving. On the morning of his eye appointment, John suffered a slight stroke and had to be hospitalized — a stroke brought on, so Bob believes, by anxiety about the prospective loss of his independence. As John recovered from his stroke, the family doctor told Bob that his father should no longer live alone. Bob and his wife held a quick family conference, and when John was ready to be discharged from the hospital, they invited him into their home.

After that John did not drive again for more than a year. When Bob thought it was time to go out in the car with his father to see if he could regain his driving skills, he quickly realized that John was oblivious to everything on the lefthand side of the road. A return visit to the ophthalmologist confirmed that John's stroke had blocked off half of his field of vision, which meant the end of any attempt to drive.

Before all this happened, Bob had been trying to persuade his father to sell his large house and move to a retirement community where he would not have to drive, but John had refused. Thus in the end John had no say-so at all about his future care.

How can we work with our parents to protect their lives, while at the same time helping them to retain a desirable quality of life? A physician who knows the family well, a geriatric specialist, or an ophthalmologist will often help in handling the decision when an elderly person can no longer safely drive. By talking about these matters ahead of time, both child and parent can begin considering alternatives and coming to terms with the decision when it must be made.

*   *   *

The following reflection questions may help you handle the driving decision when it comes.

How many small accidents has your parent had in the last year or two?

How often does your parent drive?

Does your parent drive in new territories regularly, or stick close to home?

How much night driving does your parent do?

How willing is your parent to have you drive when you go places together?

Can your parent obtain automobile and liability insurance at reasonable cost, or are the rates becoming prohibitive?

Do you know whether your parent is driving with ordinary insurance, or as a preferred risk?

Does your town or city have good public transportation?

If so, does the public-transport system include special services for the elderly?

If your elderly relative must give up driving, who is available to help with transportation needs?

"I Cook Everything at 500° ."

The occasion was a Fourth of July symphony concert in the park — a beautiful, balmy evening. Before the concert we were attending a fancy-shmancy buffet dinner for 150 people, at a private club overlooking the lake. I had my filled plate in my hand when an acquaintance came up to me and began talking about his mother.

Roland's mother was in her 80s. The day before, around dinnertime, Roland had gone over to her place and happened to notice smoke seeping from the oven door. On closer inspection, he saw that the oven was set at 500°.

"What's in the stove, Mother?" was the natural question.

"My supper," she replied.

Fearing that her supper would soon be cinders, he asked, "Why do you have the oven set at 500°?"

"Oh, I always cook everything at 500°," she airily replied. "Things get done faster that way."

The pained look on Roland's face spoke volumes: "What am I going to do?" I told him about the caregivers we had found for my mother and offered to share information about the agency that had proved to be our greatest single resource. Roland's face relaxed. He smiled and thanked me. I think both of us knew that his challenges had only just begun.

Susan had a similar experience with Carrie, her mother, who lived in an adjoining state. After Carrie had a serious fall, Carrie's doctor told Susan that her mother needed to be where a family member could attend to her welfare. So Susan and her husband moved Carrie into a comfortable cottage in the same block with their own house and put her former home on the market. Carrie seemed satisfied with this plan.

However, after Carrie's move was made, Susan took Carrie to the grocery store to help her stock her pantry and found that her mom didn't seem to know what to buy. Susan mentioned cans of soup, bread for sandwiches, breakfast cereal. Yet Carrie behaved as if all of this were a foreign concept to her. Susan finally said, "Mother, suppose we make sure you have cereal and other things for your breakfast, and then you can come to our house for your lunch and evening meal." She was thinking, *This certainly isn't what I had in mind when I brought Mother here to live.*

The next day Susan realized they were in even deeper trouble, because Carrie phoned her several times asking how to turn the lights off and on. Susan patiently told her mother that the wall switches controlled the lights, but Carrie could not grasp the idea. The can opener was the next insurmountable obstacle. Susan knew then that something was seriously wrong and had the wisdom to begin working on finding more assistance for her mother, so that the whole burden would not be hers to bear.

In another family, Ira knew that his mother was in trouble when, during a visit to his home, she asked innocently, "Have you heard anything lately from your Uncle Joel?" Ira shuddered, knowing that Joel, his mother's oldest brother, had been dead for 30 years. The sense of foreboding his mother's simple question brought on was so great that Ira simply ignored it and went on behaving as if nothing had changed.

This is often how it starts. An older person begins to do something just a little bit differently from the way he or she always did it before, or makes some remark that lets you know the rules of the game have suddenly changed. Such an event is the first sign that a parent is starting to need help — when the adult child first becomes alarmed, when responsible family members begin to scramble, when some or all of them start to become afraid. This is the moment when we know for sure that our parents will not live forever and wonder how we will cope with that reality.

This is the beginning, and it can come out of nowhere. One day things seem fine, and the next day we notice that something is not right. This is how it happens, and the change may be an irreversible and permanent one. So we do well to accept the probability that such a thing may occur and prepare ourselves for it, if and when it comes.

"I Have My Hands Full With My Own Kids. I Can't Take On Dad, Too."

Are you in the sandwich generation? Do you have children at home who take up a lot of your time, while your parents are also needing more help from you? About two decades ago, young people began delaying having children. Consequently, more and more families find themselves in sandwich situations today. Baby-boomers' parents need help as they age, yet those same baby-boomers' children need their help as well.

Many of us have looked forward to the day when our children would leave home for the Big World and we could reclaim lives of our own. Now we suddenly find ourselves faced with dependent parents who are rapidly losing ground.

Is this your situation, and if so, how are you handling it?

Are you joyful? Few of us are.

Are you panicked? You have a lot of company.

Are you asking, "Why me?" Maybe the question should be, "Why *not* me?"

If you are the only one of your parents' offspring in this predicament, are you hoping your siblings will take that into consideration and not even broach the topic with you? Dream on!

Do you believe that your time and energy need to go to your children and spouse? Have you talked with your children about that? How do they feel? If they are teenagers or in their early 20s, they may be just as happy if you have a little *less* time to focus on them.

The family members with the fullest plates are generally the ones who take on still more responsibility, probably because they do things efficiently and well. Every family must work out these arrangements differently. The first step is facing the reality, then thinking creatively of possible solutions.

Someone who has never had the day-to-day responsibility of caring for children may be less well prepared to assume such responsibilities for an elderly person. And the corollary is that families accustomed to child care are often more willing to take on the care of adults who need help. If you have children still at home, you may actually be in a better position to help with older relatives, because your children can become helpers too. Young children often enjoy being "on duty" with grandparents, as the emotional baggage that overburdens many parent-child relationships is not there. Families can be brought closer together by involving everyone in eldercare, lightening the load for all, while providing a newfound sense of extended family.

If you take on the responsibility of caring for your own parents, you are sending your children an important, positive message they will remember in years to come, when they are the ones in control.

When no one in the family is able to offer the elderly person a home, perhaps a trustworthy friend may be willing to share accommodations, expenses, and care. If this is the case, by all means encourage and support the new arrangement, rather than guiltily berating yourself because you are not able to open your own home. The happiest situation is the best situation, whatever it may be.

What are the choices for your family?

Everybody's Got To Be Somewhere

"Where is my aging parent going to live?" If you are asking yourself that question, then you must have options many people do not have. Obvious choices are their home, your home, the home of one of your siblings (if you have any) or another relative, a retirement community, a nursing home, or perhaps combining forces with a friend.

Most families make these choices cooperatively, but some adult children must face them alone. In my experience, such decisions are often made fairly quickly, usually by just a few members of the family. Money and emotions generally play the largest roles in the decision. The more money the parent has, the more choices there are. The stronger the emotional attachment between parent and child, the more likely it is that the child will go the extra miles to get that parent into the best possible environment.

*   *   *

The following questions may help you to think constructively about your own family's plan:

Is there enough money for live-in help?
Is there an acceptable retirement community close to where your
    parent has been living?
If not, is there one near where you live?
Can your parent afford to move to such a facility?
If not, does the facility offer any "scholarship" funds?
How near your parent do you want to be?
Is your parent willing to move in order to be nearer you?
Can your parent afford to buy a nice place of her own?
Is an assisted-care facility a possibility?
Do you think a nursing home may be required?
How much time and energy are you willing to put into your
    parent's care?
How flexible is your work schedule?
Have you a partner who is able and willing to help with the
    daily care your relative requires?

Probably you already know the answers to these questions, based primarily upon your and your parent's financial resources and emotional reactions.

Who Will Assume Chief Responsibility for Day-to-Day Care?

In America today, family members bear the biggest share of responsibility for frail elders. This is true even though families are often widely scattered, and elderly persons usually attempt to continue living independently as long as they can. But when savings are nonexistent, or gone, or the person becomes unable to continue living independently, family members must shoulder the load. Private resources and government aid usually do not begin to cover the overall costs of long-term care and necessities, once an older person becomes incapacitated and can no longer work.

Presently, about 8.5 million older Americans need help, help that must come from about 22.4 million families — roughly one family in three. Over the next 30 years, as baby-boomers age, the need for such family care will increase substantially. Experts tell us that the greatest potential threat to aging Americans and their families is the lack of long-term care coverage, either private or public. Today, with average annual nursing-home costs edging past $40,000 nationwide, and full-time home care costing even more, few families are ready to deal with such realities.

One couple — Tom and Julie — were both only children. Just as their own three children were moving into adolescence, both Tom's and Julie's elderly parents began to need help. Tom's salary was not a magnificent one, and after their marriage Julie had elected to be an at-home mom until their children left for college. Now, suddenly faced with four elderly relatives who had no other way of making it, Tom and Julie bit the bullet, taking all four into their home. And there they cared for all four of their parents until, one by one, the parents died or had to move to a hospital or nursing home.

Looking back on it recently, Julie laughed. "I don't know how we managed. I suppose keeping our sense of humor was what pulled us through. This house has just four bedrooms and two baths, one up and one down. Our girls moved into one room, and each set of grandparents moved into one of the other two, and Tom and I had the fourth, while our son Andy willingly slept on the sofa in the den for a couple of years. We were very lucky to have had such understanding, big-hearted kids."

Julie's friend marveled at the wonderful spirit Julie and Tom had displayed. "I don't believe I could have done what the two of you did," she said.

"Well, we were younger then," said Julie, "and we lived with the situation absolutely one day at a time." She laughed again. "Mealtimes were something else, though. If one or two of the grandparents didn't knock over a glass of something, one of the kids did. At one point Tom threatened to have a big sheet-metal trough made for our dining-room table with a drain in the middle, so all the spills would run right on through."

*   *   *

Fortunately, very few of us are faced with such a drastic eventuality as that. You may want to use the following questions to begin setting up your own family's plan for caring for elderly relatives, either now or when the time comes.

How much do you know about your elderly family members' financial resources?

Has anyone discussed long-term care? If so, is there any consensus?

What part do you see yourself playing?

Who else do you expect to participate in the plan?

What is your family's history of caring for elderly members?

What happened to your grandparents?

How often did your parents visit their parents? Where and how did each of your grandparents die?

How do you think decisions about caring for your elderly family members will be made?

What feelings have you been aware of as you answered these questions?

"This Is The Hand I Have Been Dealt."

So much depends upon our own attitude when it comes to taking care of our elders. Often, as I looked after my mother, my thoughts ran like this: "There is one world out there, and another world in here. I can be in both worlds." Such thinking gave me peace.

At other times I would think, "This is the hand I have been dealt, and I will play it to the best of my ability." Such thinking frequently got me through difficult situations. It sounds simpler than it is. But I saw early on that my own attitude had a tremendous impact on how I dealt with any given situation. Furthermore, I came to see that every situation contained a lesson for me, and I resolved to learn that lesson as fully as I could.

In truth, I was not prepared to fulfill the responsibility that ultimately fell upon me. Even though I had very clear memories of my parents' attentions to their own aging parents, their situations were very different from mine. My father's mother died suddenly of a massive heart attack, having never had any major health problems before. My mother's mother declined more gradually, her memory deteriorating. Because my mother was caring for my terminally ill father at the time and could not manage both, that grandmother had to be cared for in a nursing home in the community where she had always lived.

Looking back now, I know that one of my mother's greatest fears was that we might place her in a nursing home. This fear must have stemmed from the necessity she had faced of choosing this option for her mother. No amount of reassurance on this subject helped. My mother made it very clear to my brother and me that she expected home care, just as she had provided it for us as we grew up. And she prevailed, for, in spite of all the challenges I faced in caring for her, I never came close to moving her to a nursing home for good.

Other families have different situations, different traditions. In some instances there is no alternative to a nursing home or assisted-care facility, or even hospitalization. Whatever the decision, family traditions and examples set by previous generations exert great influence.

*   *   *

Reflecting upon the following factors may help you examine your own family history, to see what issues you face.

My grandparents were cared for by:
My partner's grandparents were cared for by:
When I was a child, my parents provided the following kind of care for me:
If I could handle this situation exactly as I chose, I would:
My family's current situation looks like this to me:
When I think about what is going on here, I experience the following feelings:
The person I can most easily talk to about this is:

"Now That Mom Needs Help, I Need Your Help Financially."

Fred vividly remembers a meeting he had with his mother and the family accountant. Fred's mother had worked hard and lived carefully her whole life, preparing well for her twilight years. Yet after the accountant had reviewed her holdings and her income, Fred's mother asked, "How much is enough?" "That is a very good question," the accountant replied. How much, indeed?

Once it is clear that an elderly person needs help, everyone wonders where the money will come from to keep him or her living as well as possible. Social Security or pension income may play a small part, but adult children are the most likely source, which can lead to difficulties. Deciding how Mom or Dad will be taken care of can test the family to its limits.

Even though Dorothy and her husband had three young children and another on the way, they agreed to take Dorothy's deaf grandmother into their household. Predictably, the arrangement soon fell apart, and Grandma was moved to a sister's home. But because the sister was elderly as well, this second plan also failed. Eventually Dorothy made a proposal to other members of the family, offering to take Grandma back if a way could be found to add on to her house, and if other family members agreed up front to help financially. Given the choice between Dorothy's offer and taking on Grandma themselves, the others willingly agreed. Everyone was a winner with this plan, and Grandma lived out her final years surrounded by loving family members.

A very workable solution for some families is having the elderly person spend time in several households for stays varying from weeks to months. In this arrangement, more people participate in the care, distributing the financial burden among all the households. If the elderly person has an income, she or he may enjoy sharing it with the host families.

In one such family, Grannie Lucy's next visit to the home of either of her two daughters was eagerly awaited. The daughters and their spouses welcomed a live-in baby sitter, and the grandchildren loved it that Grannie Lucy had time to mend their clothes, bake special treats, call out the children's spelling words, and do other small but special things to let them know she cared for them all. This woman's noninterfering temperament also had much to do with her welcome, for she never took sides in family conflicts but simply listened, watched, and said a reconciling word whenever she could. Although Grannie Lucy's presence was not essential to either household, she was loved and deeply appreciated in both.

By another creative arrangement, one member of the younger generation can shoulder primary responsibility for daily care, while other family members (including the elder one, if feasible) can contribute financially. In this case, the wider family's support may allow the primary caregiver to give up outside employment. Other families offer supplemental help to make day care or respite care available, enabling the main caregiver to either retain an outside job or maintain a fairly normal schedule in other ways.

After being widowed, Mabel gradually began to show signs of senility, so that her family of four sons and a daughter had to work out a plan. The son who was good with figures set up a custodial account and deposited all Mabel's income — from her husband's life insurance, investments she and he had made, and rental and eventually sale of her home — into that account. Mabel's daughter Nancy took their mother into her own home to look after her, receiving periodic checks from the bank account to cover Mabel's expenses.

Eventually Mabel's dementia became so severe that Nancy could not manage her at home. The siblings then agreed to place their mother in a nearby church-supported nursing home. Again, the custodial account paid the bills, and the sons supplemented the fund with their own contributions when necessary, while Nancy made sure that their mother received suitable care.

Soon, after Mabel lost the power to speak or do anything at all for herself, Nancy was spending more and more time at the nursing home to see that everything was done for her mother. When she learned that a friend with a disabled husband needed additional income, Nancy engaged this young woman to come to the nursing home and look after her mother during the daytime hours — a creative solution that worked well. And when Mabel finally died, this young woman grieved along with Mabel's family, for she had come to feel a deep affection for Mabel.

*   *   *

Answering the questions that follow may help you decide which arrangement is best for you.

Are you financially able to assume total responsibility for the elderly person?

Does the elderly person have sufficient income or assets to cover expenses?

What other family members are willing to help finance the necessary care?

What changes, if any, would you need to make in your home in order to take in your elderly relative?

How would you have to modify your schedule to accommodate an elderly person living with you?

Who in the family has enough space to take this person in?

Is it possible to pass the person around?

Time, Energy, Money, & Emotions

If I were to classify the four areas of life affected by eldercare, I would choose time, energy, money, and emotions.

We are a nation in a hurry. Fax machines and e-mail are rapidly replacing snail-mail. Cellular phones have created such a need for additional numbers that new area codes are springing up everywhere. Families rush from one activity to the next. Children stay up later at night. Supermarkets are crowded at 10:00 p.m., when two decades ago none was even open at that hour. Fast-food restaurants are everywhere. Washing machines have speed cycles, as do dishwashers and carwashes. And yet every day still has just 24 hours, the same number a day has always had. It is all about time. Yet I often wonder: are we just going nowhere, fast? It behooves every family to take a look at how we spend our time, how happy we are about our pursuits, how rich our quality of life may be.

Doing so is especially important if you are dealing with eldercare, because eldercare takes time. Where will that extra time come from? To figure out the answer, you may need to take a few minutes to reflect. What are you spending time on that you are willing to let go? Are you "wasting" time flipping through TV channels, or shopping when you don't really need anything, or in some other activity, when you could spend that time nurturing someone else?

On the topic of time, Loretta Starr's essay "Walking with Uncle Bill" offers valuable food for thought.

＊   ＊   ＊

$\mathcal{W}$ALKING WITH UNCLE BILL

Uncle Bill had had several small strokes and two heart attacks, and now that he was able to travel, we had been busy preparing for his visit to us. Because he couldn't climb the steps, we cleared out the sunroom and brought a bed down from upstairs to give him a little private space in our home. We knew that he would need resting time during the day.

It was my job to pick him up at the airport. I parked as close to the terminal entrance as I could and went inside to get him. Finally I spotted him, standing at the side of the crowd with an airport attendant and his suitcase.

"Hi, Sis," he said, with tears welling up in his eyes. He gave me a big hug, and there was no mistaking how glad he was to be with us. I picked up his suitcase and he took firm hold of his walker. "The car's just over here," I said, as I started moving slowly toward the door . . .

Always having been a fast walker, I knew that Uncle Bill would not be able to keep pace with me, so I slowed down markedly. Six steps later, I saw that Uncle Bill wasn't with me. I stopped and went back. Obviously even my slow speed was too fast. I needed to slow down further yet, so I walked with each step carefully considered. And still my pace was too fast for Uncle Bill. I had to slow down to what seemed literally a snail's pace.

I began to feel impatient. What we were doing — half a step, pause, half a step, pause — could hardly be called walking. My Results-Oriented Self was silently screaming, "We'll never get there at this rate. You'll be stuck shuffling down the concourse forever!" But another, wiser part of me also answered silently, "Quiet! You aren't in charge here."

"Shuffle" was the only description for Uncle Bill's pace. He would move his left foot forward about three inches, bump his walker forward the same amount, then bring his right foot even with his left. About every fourth step he would stop to make an observation about the airport, his flight, or the weather back in Michigan. I felt irritated at that too.

Inwardly I moaned, "Oh, Lord!" I don't know if it was a prayer or a blasphemy, but The Lord answered. "He has to stop and rest. Just relax and go with it. You aren't late for anything. What's your problem?"

Indeed, what was my hurry? I had all afternoon to get Uncle Bill to the car. If it took that long, what did it matter? I began moving at my own three inches per step, pausing between shuffles so as not to race ahead. I had to concentrate on not moving. Walking that slowly was hard work. I had to continually monitor my impatience and stop every few steps to wait for Uncle Bill to catch up. No matter how hard I tried, I could not walk as slowly as Bill.

Eventually we did reach the car, and eventually we got Uncle Bill settled at our house. His visit went well, although when we took him back to the airport for his trip back home, we made sure that a wheelchair was on hand.

That first walk with Uncle Bill continues to teach me. I know now that when I am called to be with someone in ministry, I am called to walk at the other person's pace. When I find myself impatient because I think the other person is moving too slowly, or frustrated because the other keeps running ahead, I know that I need to search within myself for whatever is demanding that the other move at my speed. Walking with Uncle Bill gave me a glimpse of my compulsiveness, the demands I make on myself and others, my need for excitement and "getting somewhere."

Walking with Uncle Bill was not fun. It was boring, and in our society, being bored is the worst of all possible worlds. Yet I know now that Christ sometimes calls me to walk in place, or at least at a pace that I may find less than exciting. True servanthood is not about pleasing myself. It is about serving the other as the other needs to be served.

In addition to time, do you have the energy to involve yourself in eldercare? Where will the energy come from, if you decide to make this caring commitment? As you focus upon your overall level of energy, would you describe yourself as a person of high, low, or medium energy? Are your energy levels fairly constant, or does your energy fluctuate greatly from one day to the next, or from one season to the one that follows?

News reports tell us that most Americans are sleep-deprived to some degree, and sleep disorders affect a surprising number of us. By current estimates, approximately half of the U.S. population has trouble sleeping — the result, primarily, of stress. The way we spend our time affects our stress, sleeplessness, and energy level. We can learn to modify our activities in order to get more rest and thus refresh and reinvigorate ourselves.

Just as eldercare calls for investments of time and energy, it also calls for money. The amount depends upon many things: how close the senior lives to you, whether you plan to invite the person into your home to live, their own financial resources, and yours. Unless the elderly relative or friend can foot some of the bills, reimburse you, or pay you in some way, this new responsibility will entail expenses for you. How will you cover them? Are there others who can help? Are community resources available to supplement what you can supply?

And as for your emotions, caring for someone with whom you share a long emotional history can stir and intensify these feelings in a disturbing way. On the other hand, it can also bring joyous moments of knowing that you are doing a right and a loving thing.

Only you can evaluate your emotional freight. When "the child becomes father to the man, (or mother to the woman)" the grown-up child often experiences many emotional ups and downs. You may already be experiencing them. If simply reading the topic for this chapter sent you into a tizzy, it is good that you are taking note of this issue now. As you have thought about the time you may or may not have at your disposal, your energy level, and the available financial resources, your emotions may have become quite highly charged. What are you feeling as you contemplate this major change in your life?

HAVING AND GETTING WHAT IT TAKES

Arriving at some kind of relative assessment of these important four areas may be helpful in your situation. Try assigning a value from 1 (lowest) to 10 (highest) to each of the areas listed below, as a way of evaluating your readiness for the task, or to indicate areas that may need some attention for better solutions.

TIME	1	2	3	4	5	6	7	8	9	10
ENERGY	1	2	3	4	5	6	7	8	9	10
MONEY	1	2	3	4	5	6	7	8	9	10
EMOTIONS	1	2	3	4	5	6	7	8	9	10

Where are your greatest strengths?
Where do you believe you will need the most improvement, or the most help?
How do you see yourself getting the help that you need?

Do We Need A Legal Eagle?

Probably. Estate planning, guardianship concerns, health-care proxies or living wills, transfer or conservation of assets — such issues can be clarified once the legal position is known.

*   *   *

Here are a few questions to help you assess the need in your particular situation.

What is the size of my parent's or parents' estate?
Whose name are the assets in?
Does my parent have a will that is valid for the state in which he or she resides?
How much do I know about my elderly relative's wishes?
Do I know how my elderly relatives want their health issues dealt with?
Does my relative have a Living Will?
Are the doctors and other health-care providers cooperating with the senior's wishes?

Does anyone have a binding Power of Attorney?
At this point, should someone be named Guardian for this person
    I care about?
Has my parent set up a trust, or is she or he the beneficiary of
    one?
Is my parent already gifting money away, as the law allows?

*   *   *

However awkward these discussions may feel, it is never too soon to have them. Some parents choose to begin gifting money to each descendant at an early stage, usually annually. Others — probably the majority — hang on to every penny like grim death. If your parent is one who may make financial matters difficult, better find that out sooner rather than later, so strategies can be devised.

Some people set up trusts to cover all monetary decisions before they die. Others add their children's names to their various holdings so that the properties will no longer be part of the estate. But because inheritance laws change from time to time and vary from state to state, sound legal advice is needed before any such arrangements are made.

Health-care issues are the ones family members usually find hardest to discuss, harder even than the financial issues. Many states allow persons to draft both a Living Will and a Health-Care Proxy, so that their wishes may be taken into account in catastrophic circumstances. Making such decisions before a crisis occurs is by far the easiest way. A sample Living Will and Health-Care Proxy are included in the Appendix to this book, and similar forms are readily available at stationery, office-supply, or book stores, or on the Internet. A reputable attorney may be necessary to assist in integrating these aspects of eldercare for you.

Making Peace With Our Parents

Watching our parents age can bring on conflicts in our feelings. Some of us may still want or need our parent to take care of us. This can be true if the parent has *always* been there for us, and it can also be true if the parent was *not* always there for us. Either we want that feeling of security to continue forever, or else we hope past hope that it is not too late to get it.

The bond between parent and child is the strongest bond in this life. If the desired relationship was not present before, as the parent ages, chances diminish with each passing day for the "perfect" dreamed-of parent-child relationship to become a reality. If I have been one of those hoping and still not getting, I may find myself in the last-chance category.

So long as both parent and adult child are willing to try to resolve old issues, it is never too late for healing. Whatever time is left *can* be more harmonious than past times. Many adults have spent much of their lives harboring resentment about things that their parents did or did not do. Yet even at a late date, if they can address these feelings in order to work through and beyond them, the relationship can improve. Are you holding on to old anger or resentments where your parent is concerned?

If you feel that you may be doing so, here are a few simple suggestions. Try making a list of everything you are angry about — a simple list, no need for great detail. Some people compose this list by means of the computer word-processor. Others keep a notebook handy, jotting things down as they remember them. If you are making such a list, be sure that you are not censoring yourself. No one else need see it. You don't have to share it with anyone. The important thing is simply being honest about what is important to you. Details don't matter. Just make your list as complete as you can, without getting perfectionistic.

One good way of accessing your anger/resentment triggers is to begin with preschool years, move on through the elementary grades, middle school, high school, college, young adulthood, partnerships, even into the years when your own children came onto the scene, middle age, the present, or whatever time line makes sense for you. Some incidents may surface that you didn't even realize you were still angry or resentful about.

Did your parents promise to take you somewhere when you were young but never kept that promise? Did they buy something for your brother or sister that you had to buy for yourself? Are you angry that you had to share your parents' love with brothers or sisters? Are your parents divorced, and do you harbor anger believing one of them cheated on or mistreated the other?

Did one or both of your parents abuse the other parent, you, your siblings, or all of you? Was there physical, emotional, sexual, financial, or spiritual abuse anywhere in your family? Any or all of these situations can lead to smoldering anger.

Now comes the second step: what you do with your list. You can write a letter to your parent including all these things, then burn, shred, or otherwise destroy it. You can carry out a ritual by which you recite the articles on your list aloud one by one, then declare after each one, also aloud, "I forgive my parent for this, and I release my resentment." Some people find it useful to do some physical activity that works their "striking back" muscles — the back, shoulder, and arm muscles. Pounding a pillow will work. So will hitting a punching bag, or shadow boxing, or pounding your arms on the water in a swimming pool. Others rake leaves, knead bread, iron, vacuum, shred paper, or twist a towel. Anything that works the back and arm muscles is helpful. You can row a boat or a rowing machine, "draw" big circles in the air with your arms in turn, or hit a tennis ball against a backboard.

Jo Ann found it helpful to rake all the autumn leaves together in her yard, making up a prayer-song about forgiveness to sing as she raked, then burning the leaves and burning her anger list on the leaf pile. Be as creative as you can in coming up with your idea. If you are doing a physical activity, just be certain that you work both sides of your body in turn. And continue the activity long enough that you want to say, "Whew!" You may have to work at it many times daily, for many days or weeks.

Are you thinking that this is silly, or too much trouble? Facing old anger and resentments, then releasing them, is *extremely* important for all of us. A wise saying is sometimes quoted: "If you don't deal with your feelings, your feelings will deal with you." Unresolved anger and resentment will always stand between you and your parents, making compassionate eldercare all the more difficult. The ghosts of the past exercise their power forever, unless they are laid to rest. Getting beyond these self-destructive feelings will make for a better life.

Another method that may work for some of us is visualizing yourself face-to-face with your parent, "telling" him or her everything that you have always wanted to say but didn't dare.

Others may actually talk to their parents directly, saying something like this: "I know things haven't always been completely right between us, and I'm unhappy about that. Starting now, I want every day to be a good day for us. I would like to tell you about some of the painful feelings I've been hanging on to from the past, because I believe that then they will lose their power to harm our relationship. Will you listen to me and then tell me some of your feelings in return?"

Wanting very much to have such a conversation with her mother, while knowing that it would be a challenge, Elaine actually wrote down those exact words on a little card, then asked her mother if she could read something important to her. By doing so, she made sure that she wouldn't lose her nerve and fall back to the status quo. Of course, if you are willing to make the effort, the parent must be open and willing too. If either of you is not ready, perhaps you will be a few days, weeks, or months from now. People *can* change, given an opportunity. You may be surprised.

A word of caution here: if your parent is drinking to excess, or misusing any drugs (prescription or otherwise), you will have little chance of mending the relationship until this basic problem is addressed. Working through this issue may best be approached with the help of a counseling professional who truly understands the operative family dynamics. One or more therapists in your area may be eager to help you, an adult child, and your parent be reconciled.

Support groups are another possibility. You may need to arrange an exploratory session with a certified addictions professional qualified to help with an intervention. Your parent's primary-care doctor may also be able to assist. One family counselor tells his client families, "While we are working together, I ask that all of you agree to abstain from alcohol and only take other medications under your doctor's supervision. I need to listen to and talk to the people, not the chemicals." The Resource section at the end of this book may guide you to competent help in your area.

If you are not able to find any support groups for adult children dealing with aging parents, you may want to start one. Your doctor, minister, hospital personnel, and nursing-home staff may be helpful in bringing together such a group.

In addition, many thousands of groups open to anyone concerned about another's use of alcohol or other drugs hold regular meetings countrywide. Faithful participation in a family group such as Al-Anon can be a tremendous help in dealing with the stresses these problems create. Almost any community, or a neighboring one, has an Al-Anon group.

"Watching My Mother Leave"

Before Nora was 8, her father abandoned his wife and child. In order to support Nora and herself, Nora's mother became a busy professional woman. Thereafter, in the mornings, little Nora would stand sadly at the front window and watch her mother leave for work. Even though Nora's mother had arranged for an able and loving caregiver to be with her daughter, Nora always felt a tug at her heart as she watched her mother leave. It was that way every morning, and even worse on mornings when Nora got up to find that her mother had already left for some important meeting or other. The mother's professional absences were sometimes as long as a week or two — an eternity to the little girl.

After Nora grew up and her mother began growing old, at first Nora didn't understand why she was feeling so terribly sad. Then it came to her. Over the months and years as her mother went slowly but steadily downhill, Nora again felt exactly like that little girl standing sadly by the window, abandoned by her father, and now also watching her mother leave. Every day her feelings were the same — the old, painfully familiar tug at her heart.

Nora was mature enough to realize that the changes in her mother were not going to reverse themselves. Some days she saw little change. On other days, a big change might have occurred — just like those long-ago mornings when Nora got up to discover that her mother had already gone. For nearly ten years it was like that, and Nora found it hard, very hard.

*   *   *

What is it like for you, watching your parent age?
What do you feel?
What do you think about?
Where does it hurt in your body?

Is there a part of you that wonders how you will be in the
world without your parents?

Is there a piece of you that worries that you are not yet really
grown up?

Driving Your Saab To The Dollar Store

For any one of us who is an adult child of an alcoholic —
and we number in the millions — money is probably a very big
issue in life. That is certainly so for Leslie. Leslie has trouble
with money — but not the most common money trouble, over-
spending. Leslie finds it harder to spend money than to save it.
That is why Leslie drives her Saab to the Dollar Store.

How did this come about? Leslie's mother was critical, a
fault-finder, almost impossible to please, as well as being inclined
to spend extravagantly, causing friction in the family. On the
other hand, Leslie's dad was the nurturing parent, the one she
wanted to be most like, the one she most wanted to please. And
because he encouraged family members to save at least half of
all the money that came into the house, Leslie learned from an
early age to win favor with her beloved dad by becoming an
extra-good saver. She put her allowance, gifts of money, and
baby-sitting earnings in her top bureau drawer, folding dollar
bills and bigger bills together and stuffing them toward the back.
As Leslie grew up, there was never a time when she did not
have that little stash.

Over the years Leslie's savings habits became even stronger.
Now age 45, she has investments and a Money Market Account.
She still saves at least half of what she earns — and Leslie, a high
achiever, earns a lot — and pays cash for everything she buys.
Any purchase over $40 requires much thought and planning. It
took Leslie ages to accumulate enough money for that Saab,
even longer to give herself permission to buy it. Leslie still finds
it hard to spend money on herself, much preferring to spend
money on others.

As parents who have had conflictual relationships with their
children age, their now-adult children often run into difficulties
around money issues. Let's look at a few possibilities.

If you have always been a spender, you may be really eager
for your parents to die, or you may just be itching to get your

hands on their money. In the meantime, you may resent every penny spent on their care, because it means that much less for you to inherit. Does this statement ring any bells? Come on, be honest.

Or, if you have always been a saver, and your parents have little capital of their own, you may be afraid that you will have to bear the expenses of their care. You may have to fork out some of your own money to pay your parents' bills. If this should happen, how will you feel?

If your parents have a lot of money but have been unwilling to share it with you, do you feel resentful or fret about the taxes you will eventually have to pay when the money becomes yours?

Do you resent the fact that your parents dangle their money like a carrot on a stick, just far enough in front of you to remind you that it's there, while refusing to share it with you?

Did your parents work so hard to make their money that you harbor resentments about that? Have you ever wished that your parents, instead of working so hard to earn money, had made more time for you when you were growing up?

Did your parents get divorced? Is either of them now married to someone who may inherit money that you have always believed to be your birthright?

Do you worry about your parents being befriended by persons outside the family, who may worm their way into your parents' confidence and persuade them to leave everything to them, rather than to you?

Do you fear that your parent may use such a relationship to manipulate you into doing exactly as he or she wishes, whether you like it or not?

All these situations are real possibilities. Such things can and do happen in families.

✻　　✻　　✻

What is your parents' financial situation?

What is your own financial situation, and how does it affect your caregiving decisions around your relatives?

Is your parent willing to add your name to bank and investment accounts, to give you access to resources needed for the parent's upkeep and care?

Has your relative signed a Power of Attorney that you may use
if necessary to help him or her?
Is it possible that your parent's mental status has already deteri-
orated to the point that naming a guardian may be wise?

"You're Not Afraid of Me Any More, Are You?"

As a therapist who works with many families that include
one or more chemically dependent (alcoholic or otherwise
addicted) persons, I have coined the phrase "reciprocal enabling."
By this I mean that everyone in the family interacts with other
members so as to manipulate and control the others' behavior.

My mother did things that made it possible for my alcoholic
father to continue to drink with impunity, while my father made
allowances for my mother's volatile temper. Dad used alcohol
to control his feelings, while Mom used her temper to control
the rest of us — and, I now believe, to mask or "funnel" all her
other feelings.

As a little girl, if ever I looked as if I might be about to cry
— "tune up" were the words my mother used — I was invariably
sent to my room. Little wonder, then, that I still go to my
room whenever I feel as if I want to cry.

And if ever I appeared to be getting angry, my mother would
warn, "Now, remember, pretty is as pretty does," or "Don't be
ugly!" I certainly did not want to turn ugly, and the message I
internalized, therefore, was that I was not allowed to be angry.
And so for the first 40 years of my life, I taught myself to
repress my anger and never cried more than one tear at a time.
The result was a low-grade depression.

In therapy, at age 40 — initiated because of relationship issues
— one of my major tasks was learning how to be angry. My
therapist taught me how, and once I started allowing myself to
be angry and then release it, I understood how much anger I
had pent up inside me, and how good it felt to let it out.

One day in conversation with my mother, I began telling
her that I had gotten angry in a staff meeting and described the
encounter in detail. With a gleam in her eye, my mother replied,
"Now you're not afraid of me any more, are you?"

Such a smart woman, my mother, and how honest she could
be. Although I regretted that her need to control and my lack

of coping skills had kept me afraid for so many years, at last I had broken out of that fear. The reciprocity was gone. Never again would she attempt to control me with her anger, and never again would I cave in through fear, for now I could stand up to her and to anyone else in the face of their anger. Our relationship was different from that moment on and much better.

"Will My Friends Be There For Me?"

Can you predict how your friends will view your involvement with eldercare? All of us can speculate what we might do in a particular situation, or how we might feel, but none of us really knows how we will feel or what we will actually do when a pressing situation confronts us.

When Steve and Shirley became deeply involved in caring for Steve's elderly mother, one of their best friends was also terminally ill. They worked diligently to divide their time between the two, although whenever the friend had a bad day, it seemed that Steve's mother would usually take a turn for the worse too. Shirley and Steve hung in there, but they sometimes felt as if they were being pulled apart, emotionally and physically.

When two of their other friends asked, "Why are you doing this?" Shirley and Steve were shocked. Obviously (to them), they were doing it because they cared about two people close to them who needed their help. It came as no surprise when they later learned that the questioning husband had had no contact with his only brother for 20 years, or that his wife had little interest in or contact with her side of the family. These two couples had very different values, and over the succeeding years their friendship waned.

Others among Shirley's and Steve's friends became real players with them in their caregiving. Several volunteered to help in a variety of ways, spelling the couple in Steve's mother's final days when they really needed respite care. Those friends were the ones to whom Steve and Shirley turned, the ones who understood. These friendships have endured.

As you think of your own friends, what do you know about their lives with their immediate and extended families that might make a difference in their attitude toward eldercare? Do you have friends you can count on to be of real support to you when you need it? For example, you may often meet people in similar situations when you accompany your parent to a doctor's appointment. Your place of work or your church are other places where you may meet people in situations similar to yours. Some of these connections may blossom into truly supportive, mutually rewarding friendships.

"She's Your Mother. It's Not My Problem." (Or Is It?)

If you are married, did any portion of your marriage vows call for taking care of each other's parents? No, mine didn't either. Yet once a couple marries, chances are that either or both will eventually be involved to some extent in caring for the other partner's parents. One can only hope that the partner will be willing to help to some degree, or at least support the adult child who must help.

For some couples it's no big deal. If a marriage is going well, both partners want to be there for each other, and their handling of eldercare issues is often a good sign of the health of the partnership. For others, the issue may be more difficult. In strained marriages, eldercare matters may not go as well.

Daughters-in-law and sons-in-law can have a tremendous influence in an eldercare situation. The groundwork for their relationship with the in-law parent has already been laid. The better the in-law spouse gets along with the partner's parents, the more likely he or she will be to help, and the more likely it is that the older generation will accept that help. Yet in some families the partner would rather be strung up by the fingertips than participate in a mother- or father-in-law's care. This is especially true when the in-law parent has been unjust or inconsiderate toward the son- or daughter-in-law, or vice versa. That fact must be taken into account fairly and reasonably.

It often works best for the elderly person's daughter or son to have the final word in any decision. Even so, the son- or daughter-in-law may make the more rational decisions, because the emotional overlay may be less. The long view may be clearer to the daughter- or son-in-law, who may also find it easier to be "nice" to the parent-in-law, and more courteous than if caught up in the same situation with his or her own parent.

During my mother's care, my husband was by my side through thick and thin. We talked about everything. Whenever sticky issues came up, he was there. We worked out differences between us, and then we stood united. He did this willingly, and the rewards were immense.

After we had decided that only by hiring caregivers could I keep my career afloat and maintain my emotional well-being, at times we had trouble keeping caregivers on the job. Once when a caregiver called in sick, because we had heavy involvements of our own, we had to take my mother to a nursing home for a weekend. We explained that the measure was temporary and that I would be back on Sunday to bring her home. Angrily, Mother made it clear that she thought I was trying to deceive her. When my husband tried to mollify her, she turned angrily on him: "That's enough out of *you*, Bub!" Fortunately for all of us, he could just laugh it off. After she spent the weekend there, staff reported to us that she tried to smother another patient. Such was her dementia, and such is the difficulty of these problems.

"And, Anyway, Where's Your Darling Sister In All Of This?"

Sibling involvement, or lack of it, can often be a sore point. Once the primary caregiver is identified, others may breathe a sign of relief and decide that they need not participate. My experience is that a small subset of all the possible candidates will manage the elderly person's care, and seeking to involve others who have no interest in taking part may create more problems than it solves.

So, if the "darling sister" or "dear brother" has made it clear through absence or nonavailability that they do not intend to become players, you can only hope that they have the grace not to criticize your management of the situation. If you wish, you can communicate to that person or persons as clearly as possible what you would like to have from them: a weekly phone call or letter of encouragement and support, an occasional visit, a regular check, whatever it may be. But it is useless to get bent out of shape if the commitment of other family members is not as great as yours. Siblings very seldom share equally in eldercare.

Near the end of a father's long, slow decline, his son David came from a considerable distance for a very brief visit with his dad and sister Mary, who lived near their father and was seeing to his day-to-day care. The next day, just before leaving, David told Mary, "What Dad needs is a little outing now and then. You can come over and pick him up, take him somewhere pleasant, bring him back to the apartment. I know it would help him." Mary steamed. She held her tongue, but sarcastic words ran through her mind: "David, please come into town for 24 hours again and tell us how to run our lives."

There is an old saying, "Your son is a son 'til he takes him a wife, but your daughter's your daughter the whole of her life." In eldercare situations, it is often profoundly true. Let's suppose Mary had been able to say, "David, that's a good suggestion. I am doing all I can for Dad with the time and energy available to me. Maybe you will come again soon and stay long enough yourself to take Dad for an outing or two." By a comment like that, Mary would have released some of her frustration and offered David a concrete way to help, whether he complied or not.

You May Need To Hire Columbo

At times of particular stress — death of a spouse, retirement or loss of a job, moving to a different neighborhood or town — an elderly person sometimes reacts by drinking to excess, misusing prescription medications or other drugs, or both. An estimated 3 million older Americans are alcoholic, and as many as one in five persons over the age of 65 has some problem with alcohol. Today more older Americans are hospitalized for alcohol problems than are hospitalized for problems with their hearts. So the possibility of this happening to an elderly person close to you is not a remote one. Yet the signs can be very subtle indeed. Sometimes a "Columbo" may be needed to help you figure out what is going on.

*   *   *

What have you been noticing?

Are your parents, or is your parent, less eager to visit you?

Is the person you're concerned about less inclined to welcome you to his or her home?

Are the person's grooming and personal hygiene starting to slip?

Is your relative's home less tidy and presentable than it used to be?

Have you noticed that the person has short-term memory problems, or memory gaps?

Are you aware of any recent sleep disturbances?

Has your parent ever had an abnormal blood test, especially concerning liver function?

Does your relative seem somewhat depressed?

Is his or her kitchen stocked with nutritious food, or only with snacks and nibbles?

Is your parent crabbier than usual?

Have you ever phoned your parent late in the day or evening and noticed that his or her speech is slurred?

When your parent visits you, does he or she bring along liquor to be sure of getting a drink?

Have there been any unexplained falls? Unexplained bruises?

Is your relative reluctant to discuss certain aspects of daily life?

Does the person become angry if you bring up his or her use of alcohol or other drugs?

Is this person more secretive than in the past?

*   *   *

Your answers may suggest that your parent is drinking to excess, misusing drugs, or both. The signs are particularly hard to spot if you yourself enjoy drinking or freely use prescription medications or other drugs.

If you believe your concerns are valid, you will probably want to discuss the matter with an appropriate person — not Columbo, but perhaps an addictions professional who can help you evaluate your options. If you don't know where to turn, a call to the National Council on Alcohol and Drug Dependence (1-800-NCA-CALL) can guide you to appropriate help.

Maureen and Tim are the adult children of Dr. M., a well-respected retired professional, and his wife. Brother and sister, both alcoholic, were already in recovery programs when their parents' health began to fail. Mrs. M., an obese overeater, had several falls and finally was hospitalized when her debilitated husband proved unable to care for her at home.

Nevertheless, Dr. M. was at his wife's side in the hospital day and night, having brought along several prescription bottles. He was intent on seeing that his wife took these medications every day. After the attending doctors were unable to reach a conclusive diagnosis, one of them asked Dr. M. if he had brought all his wife's medications to the hospital. "No, not all," he said. "I would need a U-Haul to bring in everything that's been prescribed."

Maureen and Tim went to the house to investigate and were shocked to discover an entire kitchen cabinet — three shelves — full of prescription drugs. Mrs. M. had been helping herself for years to a pharmaceutical smorgasbord. No wonder the dear lady was falling down.

Tim and Maureen realized that they had been "not seeing" what was going on in their parents' home. After a long talk with the doctors, it came out that both Dr. and Mrs. M. had been misusing alcohol and prescription drugs for decades, each covering up for the other. Once the family secret was out, their children could take steps to arrange for the supervision and care that both parents required.

*   *   *

Do you know what medications have been prescribed for your parent or relative?

Do all the doctors who care for this person know about all the medications prescribed?

Does the pharmacist who fills the prescriptions know of all the medications the person takes?

Has more than one pharmacy been filling prescriptions for your relative?

Do you know whether your relative drinks?

Do you know what, how often, and how much? Do your parent's doctor(s) and pharmacist(s) know about your relative's drinking habits?

What precautions are in place to guard against irresponsible use of alcohol or other drugs?

If there is a chemical problem, will you discuss the matter with the involved health-care professionals and work out appropriate solutions?

"What Do I Do For Lunch?"

The line between functional and nonfunctional living can be as clear as a phone call. Sally's mother, Martha, had been living in an apartment a few blocks from her daughter for several years. She routinely shopped, cooked, and kept house for herself. Sally had been noticing that recently her mother seemed a bit more withdrawn, less willing to go places or do things without Sally, and totally resistant to all major undertakings. But the reality of her decline became truly clear on the day that Martha phoned Sally and asked innocently, "What do I do for lunch?"

Before the question was asked, Sally had begun to wonder whether her mother was eating regular nutritious meals. Now, in the wake of the phone call, Sally stood looking out the window with a sense of fear and dread, knowing that life would never again be the same. At some deep level she knew that the course of her life, and Martha's, had changed in a major way.

Martha's doctor, an astute young geriatric specialist, diagnosed "a blackout." "What is that?" asked Sally. To her surprise, the doctor replied, "A period of amnesia, brought on by drinking." The doctor had already told Sally that Martha did not appear to be a typical Alzheimer's patient. Her next question was, "How much does your mother drink?"

Sally could not answer, although she had always known that her mother drank "socially." She had never heard her mother speak with even the slightest slur in her speech, never had any reason to be concerned. Now, however, she recalled that after Martha moved to be nearer Sally, while they were unpacking the boxes, *seven* had turned out to be full cases of liquor — most unusual for a retired elderly widow who would not be planning any large-scale entertaining. Sally had seen, but she had also not seen.

Then there was the fall Martha took soon after the move, and the overturned card table in her TV room with little spots that could have been dried red wine. Splotches were appearing on her skin, and recent abnormal blood tests could not be explained. When Sally questioned the neighbor who took Martha grocery shopping every week, she learned that her mother invariably bought quantities of wine. The puzzle had come together. Martha was alcoholic.

Her doctor confirmed this for Sally and offered to hospitalize Martha for detoxification. Sally feared that a strange new environment would only add to her mother's disorientation. She and the doctor therefore agreed to keep Martha on a maintenance level of alcohol until they could arrange to have someone with her 24 hours a day to supervise her medication while attempting to detoxify her.

So Sally found herself buying small amounts of alcohol for her mother every few days. It was a strange feeling. She had never expected to be buying her mother booze. The detox problem was solved after Sally's brother and his family agreed to come at Christmas and stay for a week. They came, Martha was glad to see them, and the plan succeeded, although Martha had a somewhat sedated Christmas season that year. Sally took over all the grocery shopping, eliminating the wine.

Soon Martha's blood tests returned to normal, and the skin splotches began to disappear. For a while it appeared that there had been a "miracle cure." But then, ever so slowly, other signs of dementia appeared. The geriatrician and a local addictionologist (medical specialist in addictions) agreed that alcoholism was the cause — the creeping kind.

Martha's drinking had begun innocently — an occasional Scotch-and-water with friends, maintained at that level for at least four decades, maybe half a century. And then, when she was alone, widowed, retired, and trying to adapt to a new environment, her disease gained enough momentum to cause irreparable harm. Sally wonders now how many elderly people with the same disease have been misdiagnosed.

If Your Parent Has Alcoholism, Congratulations! You Are An Adult Child of An Alcoholic.

What's your first response to that? Is it "So what?" Do you shudder with horror? Or do you think, "Well, this is my parent's problem. It has very little to do with me." Do you have some entirely different reaction?

If you already know that a parent has the disease of alcoholism, you may also be aware of the extensive literature available on the topic. Furthermore, you may already accept the well-founded possibility that you have an inborn genetic predisposition to the same disease yourself. But if you are just coming to terms with your parent's illness, you may not know that you have undoubtedly taken on certain predictable attitudes and behavioral characteristics just from growing up in a home affected by addictive disease.

The same thing can happen even in homes where neither parent has alcoholism, if one or more of the grandparents suffered from the disease, or an aunt or uncle, a brother or a sister. Behavioral patterns are passed down through the generations, and the unspoken rules that dominate families affected by alcoholism or other addictions may be a part of your personal heritage, if anyone in your family tree has or had the disease.

I was about 40 when I realized that I was an adult child of an alcoholic (ACOA), or rather, of two alcoholics. I had entered therapy because, after ending a relationship, I felt better, oddly enough, than I had felt for a long time. And that was not the first time. The same thing had happened three times. I began to see what I viewed as a "mistake pattern," and I wanted to know how to break it up.

As I got to know other ACOAs, all of us realized we had grown up with a "No Talk" rule. We had never talked much within the family or outside it about our home life. In addition, we discovered that we all found it difficult to trust others or to trust life in general. Finally, we had the greatest difficulty in expressing feelings. Some of us didn't even know what our true feelings were. One woman often had to consult a list of feelings to help her name what she felt.

My newfound friends and I also learned that we had slid into roles in our families. Some were the family's Heroes — first on the scene to help others, hard workers, and often big successes in whatever line of work we had taken up. Others had been the family's Troublemakers, or Scapegoats — some in trouble with the law, some expelled from school, some with unwanted pregnancies, some falling into alcoholism or other-drug addiction themselves. Other ACOAs had simply lived lives of loneliness — living out the family role of the Lost Child. This group felt that their families hardly knew they existed, and even as adults they often faded into the woodwork. The last group described themselves as Clowns, or Mischief Makers. Often the center of attention in their families, they became the class clowns at school and maintained this role in adult life. How many famous comedians, I wonder, have been their family's Clowns?

In some families, one person may carry more than one role. The Troublemaker may also be the Family Clown. Or the Scapegoat may adopt some of the defenses of the Lost Child. Perhaps the person most deserving of our compassion is the only child in a household affected by alcoholism, who for purposes of survival may adopt pieces of all the possible roles.

Eventually we learned that we all shared similar feelings and used our adopted role-behaviors as defense mechanisms to cover up our pain. Whenever we felt angry, ashamed, embarrassed, or sad, we didn't know how to handle such feelings, and so we adopted role-behaviors that protected us, at least for a time.

Slowly but surely, as many of us moved through recovery, we shed those defenses and became able to express at least some of our feelings. We began to talk, trust, and feel all kinds of emotions that had previously been unavailable to us.

*   *   *

You may want to take a few minutes now and make some notes about how such patterns might affect you, and where you may be in this process.

Is there a situation in your family, or was there one in the past, about which you have felt angry?

What was it? How do or did you handle that anger?

Is there anything about your family around which you feel shame? Again, what is it? How did you handle it?

Is there anything about your family that used to embarrass you, or embarrasses you still? Did you pay attention to your feelings? What did you do about it?

When you think about your family now, do you ever feel sad?

Was there something you wanted from your family while you
were growing up that you never got? What is it? Have you
told anybody about it?

She Smiled And Waved

Adults who grew up with alcoholic or otherwise addicted
parents have major, long-lasting issues. Consider Jeff's story.

Jeff's mother, a stay-at-home mom, had been zonked on
prescription drugs as long as Jeff could remember. He rarely
saw her except when she got out of bed to go to the bathroom
or kitchen. His dad was a successful workaholic businessman
who put in extra-long hours, often traveling for one or two
weeks at a time. Jeff's dad was also a functional alcoholic. So
young Jeff was generally left to amuse and rear himself.

A big tree stood in front of Jeff's house, clearly visible from
the kitchen window. One day 10-year-old Jeff was entertaining
himself climbing in this tree. After trying various stunts, Jeff
hung by his knees, swinging back and forth, until he realized he
could not get down on his own. Just then his mom drifted past
the kitchen window. He waved frantically at her. He needed
help! His mom smiled foggily, waved back, and wandered off to
bed again.

Twenty-five years later Jeff was still talking about that event.
How many times had similar things happened to him? How
much time must he have spent alone? Who had been there for
him, as he was growing up? Had he dealt with his undoubtedly
painful feelings, and moved beyond them? The answers seemed
obvious to me.

At age 35, Jeff, still living in the same town with his parents,
remained tied to them. Whenever they needed so much as a
light bulb changed, they called Jeff, and he came. When his own
alcoholism and other-drug dependency had kicked in in his late
teens, those parents covered up and took care of Jeff, just as he
always covered up for and took care of them. Chemical dependency was their painful family secret, and it eventually killed all
three.

Jeff's story is about not-taking-care-of, and about taking-care-
of-too-much. Do you suppose that you or your parents have
done either of these things?

"No One Else Can Do It.
They're All Drunk or Drugged."

That statement sounds like a Family Hero talking. Are you that person? Have you spent your life taking care of everyone else? Were you the one to mow the lawn as soon as you were old enough? Did you start at an early age trying to keep the house neat and clean? Were you a super athlete? Did you get top grades in school? Is your ironing done, your car maintenance up to date, and do the birthday cards you send always get there a little early? In other words, have you always worked hard to be that "perfect" child in your family?

If you are the Family Hero, very likely you are also the family caregiver, the one who automatically assumes eldercare responsibilities. It may never have occurred to you that someone else could share the burden. And you may be right.

If other family members happen to be battling addictions to alcohol or other drugs, no one can expect them to step in and become competent caregivers. However much you may wish that they would help out, allowing it would be unwise. If this is your family situation, first of all, be honest about it. It would be a mistake, for example, to depend on a drinking alcoholic to drive Mother to her doctor's appointment. Furthermore, that person might be in a blackout and simply fail to show up. If a family member is not trustworthy, just face the fact and stop belaboring the point.

Getting other members of your family to change is frankly impossible, and trying to do so would be inappropriate. But for your own peace of mind and overall health you need to be honest about your feelings concerning the way things are working out. Truthfully, do you consider your service another "jewel in your crown"? Do people sometimes ask you where you think you are going carrying that cross? Do you secretly enjoy the power you get from knowing that you are the only one who can handle the situation?

On the positive side, if you *are* the only one in the driver's seat, some aspects of eldercare are actually easier. Nobody else has to be consulted before you take action, and you don't have to deal with a whole host of differing opinions. On the negative side, anyone tires after a while if no relief driver comes in for the long haul. So that is the balancing act to be performed.

If other family members are at all open to working together to spare you the entire load, a few places offer short-term counseling that may help. Some counseling professionals are highly skilled at working with entire families. Their job is not to point out who is right and who is wrong, but rather to try to help everyone overcome the family's hang-ups in order to work out solutions.

Eldercare issues can bring siblings into contact in ways they have not been in contact in decades, and when this happens, family members usually revert to the roles, however unhelpful, that they formerly played in the family system. The Family Hero reappears, along with the Family Troublemaker. The Lost Child may now be 45 years old, still "lost." The Family Clown may try to lessen the tension by making everybody laugh, while avoiding the serious issues to be addressed.

❉   ❉   ❉

Does your family need this kind of group assistance?
If so, do you believe other family members would be receptive
    to such a plan?
Do you believe that your family has any choice?
What do you think the payoff might be?
What do you believe may happen if things remain as they are now?
How do you feel about things remaining the same?
How will you cope with the situation if nothing changes?
Where will you find assistance if other family members do not
    give their help?

"I'm The Family Scapegoat (or Clown, or Lost Child). I'll Let the Hero Do It, As Usual."

To the Family Hero, this is a maddening attitude. Roles assumed in childhood usually carry over into adulthood. Heroes become super-achievers. Scapegoats, Mascots, or Lost Children continue those same roles in adulthood, unless they find good psychotherapy, a recovery program, or both. Although everyone in the family is "used to" the roles, over time they can wear very thin, especially if *you* are the one who always assumes the onerous tasks everyone else shirks. The mere fact that you are reading this book strongly suggests that you take the role of the Hero — the automatic caretaker — in your family.

Amy, in the throes of struggling with her father's advanced alcoholism, received a call from her brother Phil. Their mother had been visiting Phil and his family for several weeks, and Phil was about to put Mom on a plane to return home. Phil began telling Amy how concerned he and his wife were to see that Mom was likewise drinking a great deal. As soon as Mom got home, he told his sister, Amy should set up some kind of plan to deal with the problem.

Of course, Phil had always been the Clown/Scapegoat, while Sis had played the Hero, with a touch of Lost Child thrown in. Phil was simply playing out his old role, sending his mother home with her problem intact, to let Sis take care of it. They had lived out this pattern for their entire lives. Sis always did the work, while Phil removed himself from the scene.

*   *   *

Your family may have some similar patterns. Can you name them?

If such patterns do exist in your family, what effect have they on your eldercare situation?

Who is the primary caregiver for the elderly person or persons in your life?

What role has this primary caregiver played in the family thus far?

What role have you played?

What are the other siblings' names? Can you say which role each of them has played?

How have the roles from childhood affected caregiving for your elders as a whole?

If there is inequity, how do you feel about it, and how are you dealing with those feelings?

Can you think of more helpful ways to deal with the situation and the feelings?

"OK, If It Is Alcohol or Drugs, Then What?"

When one member of a family misuses alcohol or other drugs, others in the family suffer the fallout. This is especially true when the drinking or drugging person is elderly and depends substantially upon other family members for care. The story can be a complicated one.

Ellen knew that she suffered from alcoholism. When she was in her late 40s and her son Scott insisted she get help, she consulted an alcoholism counselor and began regularly attending Alcoholics Anonymous. Ellen had multiple age-related health problems, however, and as these worsened, her addiction-ignorant physician prescribed tranquilizers, with refills as often as she needed them. By the time Ellen had been "in recovery" from alcoholism for 20 years, she found herself absolutely dependent upon those little yellow pills.

When Scott realized that his mother was sleeping through much of the day and staying awake for much of the night, he first satisfied himself that Ellen had not gone back to drinking, then concluded the fault lay with the tranquilizer pills. He consulted an addictions specialist who confirmed his conclusion and laid out four choices:

1. Do nothing.
2. Get help for himself through support-group meetings, such as Al-Anon or Adult Children of Alcoholics (ACOA), or a co-dependency treatment program.
3. Plan an intervention.
4. Cut off Ellen's pill supply, although that was not without its risks.

The first choice was unacceptable, and the second did not address the primary problem. Scott knew that abruptly cutting off a person's supply of alcohol or other drugs without medical supervision can endanger that person's health. He therefore chose to plan an intervention, calling on Ellen's sister, doctor, and minister to help.

The intervention was successful. Ellen, grateful somebody cared, accepted the help offered, entered a chemical-dependency treatment program, and reclaimed a full-fledged recovery. Scott decided to begin attending Al-Anon meetings himself, learning new ways to deal with life challenges and truly be of help to his mother in her later years.

Tragically, in many such situations, physicians, clergy, and family members who don't understand effective approaches to addictive disease refuse to intervene in an alcohol or drug problem when the person is elderly. "Good grief, she's in her 70s, leave her alone," someone usually says, or, "He's in his 80s, and since his wife died, the comfort of a few drinks is all he has left." This is an unnecessarily sad state of affairs. Everyone deserves the best possible chance for good health, clarity of mind, and mutually pleasurable relationships with family and friends.

Matt, a highly respected 73-year-old widower who was also a late-blooming alcoholic, habitually drove drunk, even though all the law-enforcement officers in his small town knew it. Matt's daughter Patty tried taking away the car keys, but Matt just went out and bought a new car. In desperation, Patty begged the Chief of Police to have her dad picked up when he was out in his car after his evening ration of booze. "Oh, no, ma'am," this Southern gentleman replied. "That would embarrass us and Mr. Matt to death. We could never do that. We just send out an officer to follow him home and make sure he gets there all right." How unnecessary, and how sad.

In contrast, Frank, a 76-year-old retired alcoholic surgeon whose wife and children insisted that he go through a chemical-dependency treatment program, lived to be 84, frequently telling anyone who would listen that those last eight years in sobriety had been the happiest of his life.

"My Husband Doesn't Drink."

Millie, married for ages to Walter, an alcoholic college professor, had been diagnosed in the distant past as having chronic depression. And, as was so often the case then as now, the physician in charge had prescribed mood-altering medications. Through the years that followed, Millie had her prescriptions refilled regularly, going to various pharmacies to make sure of keeping up her supply. And Walter continued to drink.

The strategy Walter had worked out was to announce several times each evening, as Millie's drug-induced stupor deepened, that he was going out to the garage to feed the cat. Eventually, after their children had grown up and left home, the cat died. Yet Walter continued his multiple evening trips to the garage, while Millie never raised an eyebrow. Finally one night after the fifth or sixth "cat-feeding" trip, Walter slipped on a throw rug and crashed heavily to the floor. Millie roused herself sufficiently to realize that he needed medical attention, and somehow the two of them made it to the local emergency room.

At the E.R. Millie waited in the hall while the physician examined Walter. "Doctor, what is wrong with my husband?" she asked, when he emerged.

"He has a broken jaw," came the reply, "and furthermore, ma'am, your husband is quite drunk!"

"Oh, no," pathetic Millie replied. "You must be mistaken. My husband doesn't drink!"

When this couple's two sons heard the details of the mishap, they had to face up to the need to arrange appropriate care for their parents. Doing so was not easy, for Walter was a revered member of the college faculty, and Millie was known as the nicest, sweetest woman in town. No one could believe that their lives were in such a muddle. The denial and self-imposed isolation that had protected these two addicted older folks also robbed them of a far more satisfying quality of life.

What could have been different? What do you think you would do, faced with a similar situation?

"If We Need An Intervention, Exactly What Is It?"

The process known as intervention was devised in the 1960s by The Reverend Vernon Johnson, an Episcopal priest. Previously, most people had believed that alcoholics or addicts had to "hit bottom" before they could be helped. Johnson came up with the life-saving concept of group pressure to "raise the bottom," persuading alcoholics or addicts to accept help before too many losses occurred in their lives. Johnson's book *Intervention: How To Help Someone Who Doesn't Want Help* outlines this powerful method, by which those who care about the alcoholic or addict are taught to present their concern in a way that the person can hear.

If you believe an intervention may be needed in your family, go ahead to plan one, but *only after you have secured trained assistance in carrying it out.* The importance of this point cannot be stressed enough. Properly done, interventions save lives. Without the right training or leadership, however, they can do tremendous harm. Today many addictions counselors, clergy, and other helping professionals have been well trained in the intervention technique. Unfortunately, others who will tell you that they understand it are not competent to facilitate an intervention.

Don't stop looking until you find a professional who has been trained in the intervention technique before you take the first step. Your local chapter of the National Council on Alcoholism and Drug Dependence can help you find such a person, or you can call 1-800-NCA-CALL for information. After that, the helping professional to whom you are referred will guide you through the process.

*   *   *

The steps of an intervention are, briefly, as follows:

1. Participants are helped to conquer their reluctance. The helping professional sees to this before any other steps are taken.
2. An intervention team gathers. Again, the trained professional decides who else should take part. This team may include a spouse or partner, children, other family members, a close friend, a member of the clergy, boss or co-workers, a physician, or anyone else with helpful knowledge of the situation.
3. The team gathers the data. The interventionist guides this process as well.
4. Everyone meets to rehearse the intervention. This step ensures that the intervention will go as planned and that resistances or difficulties can be overcome.
5. The planners wrap up all details — how to get the person to the intervention, where it will take place, what will happen afterward.
6. The team and the interventionist carry out the intervention.
7. The follow-up plan is carried through.

When an elderly person dependent on others for his or her care is the object of shared concern, chances are that the intervention will succeed. A person who needs the day-to-day support of others is not in a position to refuse help for the chemical problem. In this situation, family members have a great deal more clout than they may have had in the past. So go ahead with your intervention if necessary. It's well worth the effort. But do it with love, for anger or blaming are not successful approaches.

Leaving Mother In The Mall

Jessica's mother always phoned her the moment she needed anything — an envelope, a toothbrush, a new TV. One day she phoned saying she needed new shoes. Although Jessica despised shopping in stores, she dutifully telephoned around to find a store that carried her mother's preferred brand of shoes, then went on Sunday afternoon to take her mother to the mall.

The autumn day was one of those clear, beautiful ones when all you can think of is being in the great outdoors. Jessica hated being at the mall, but, after all, her mother wanted new shoes.

Although the shoe-store assistant was patient and polite, Jessica's mother soon worked herself into one of what Jessica called "her snits." Jessica herself was a recovering alcoholic, several years down the sobriety road. Her mother was also alcoholic but no longer drinking, through no choice of her own. She could in no way be referred to as recovering. A "dry drunk" would be a more accurate description.

So, when her mother's crabbing got to be too much, Jessica simply stood up and told her mother and the sales assistant she would be back in a few minutes. Total silence greeted her announcement. And, without looking back, Jessica walked quickly and quietly out of the store.

As she strode energetically down one side of the mall and back up the other, Jessica was able to cool off and put the situation into perspective. Ten minutes later, when she returned to the store, her mother was standing by the cash register wearing new shoes. Obviously she had made her purchase. Jessica apologized to the sales assistant for her mother's behavior, thanked him, and started walking with her mother out of the mall.

When they got into the car, Jessica's mother turned to her and said, "Sometimes I don't know why you put up with me."

Jessica responded, "Sometimes it is a real challenge." As she drove her mother home, neither of them had much to say, yet this was an important turning point in their relationship. How many cranky mothers or fathers, aunts or uncles, might shape up if they were "left in the mall" a time or two?

The Big Six: Confusion, Anger, Happiness, Sadness, Fear, & Guilt

The more balanced a person is, the more likely he or she is to be able to feel and express the Big Six emotions. And balance is surely desirable for anyone undertaking eldercare.

One who is confused and knows it can discuss the confusion in order to sort through it. Someone who knows she is angry can recognize the fact, try to discover why, and consider strategies to release and move beyond the anger. Happy people know when they are happy and are not afraid to show it, often through hearty, spontaneous laughter.

Some of us also know when we are afraid, can talk about our fear, and can acknowledge whether our fears are reality-based or otherwise. Some of us know that we have done things that do not match our values, or have acted wrongly through carelessness, and can talk about our feelings of guilt.

Unfortunately, people who possess this broad range of accessible feelings are few and far between. Much more often we find that people "funnel" their feelings. Their funnel may look something like this:

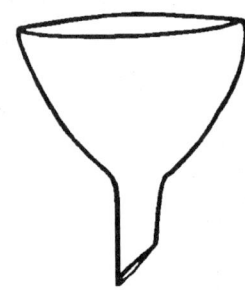

I call this coping mechanism a funnel because each and every one of us was born with the ability to express *all* human feelings. Depending upon what has happened to us throughout life and what we were given permission to express growing up, however, we may have become accustomed to funneling all of our feelings into one and blocking out the rest. We may seem to be always confused, always angry, always happy, always sad, always afraid, or always guilty. None of these conditions is a healthy way to be, for human beings need balance and emotional richness in their lives.

*   *   *

Just thinking about today, try to answer the following questions.

Which feeling did you feel and express upon waking up this morning?

As you progressed through your morning routine, what did you feel?

If you had to wait in line, or in traffic, or some other potentially frustrating situation, how did you handle it?

If you received bad news, how did you deal with it? What feeling did you express?

When was the last time you really laughed, spontaneously and heartily?

When did you last cry? How long did that crying last? Did you try to stop it, or apologize for it?

What was the last thing you felt guilty about? Did you reflect on it, or try to forget it?

How confused do you feel right now?

When you focus on the situation of your elderly relative or friend, what is the first feeling that surfaces?

*   *   *

Your answers to these questions are clues as to how much you "funnel," and how much or how little you "funnel" is a pretty reliable indicator of how you will most likely react to and cope with eldercare responsibilities.

And When She Was An Old Woman, She Wanted To Wear Old Clothes

Nancy and her mother Anne were in the doctor's office, and Mother was on the examining table. The doctor commented that Anne always wore the prettiest underwear. That day, Anne had on a chocolate-colored slip edged with ecru lace. It was indeed beautiful, and it was many years old. Nancy commented to the doctor that her mother liked to wear clothing that she had had for a long time — old clothes — despite the fact that Nancy often took her shopping or brought her new things. The doctor remarked that this was quite common.

One of Nancy's many challenges as Anne aged and became increasingly dependent upon her help was outfitting her. Anne had clothes, several closets full — formal attire, furs, and many suits and dresses that she had worn in her business life. What she lacked were comfortable, easy-to-launder clothes that fit her retired, more casual lifestyle. And she was reluctant to change. Was it her image? Did those older clothes represent her identity as a successful businesswoman? Did they evoke memories? What was it about them that she preferred?

Even her bathrobes were elegant. They were all long and lightweight, even the winter ones, with fancy trimming or other distinctive characteristics. They said something about who Anne was. Yet Nancy found that after helping her mother bathe or shower, Anne complained of being cold while Nancy was drying her off. The solution? It was so obvious. A long terry-cloth bathrobe did the trick. Anne could put it on immediately after getting out of the shower, so that it served as both bath towel and warm robe.

Sweat suits were another solution. Anne received the first one as a Christmas gift from her grandchildren. At first, although she was pleased with the gift, she was reluctant to wear it. Once into it, however, she wanted to wear it almost all the time. Nancy bought several more in a variety of colors, soft, warm, and comfortable — ideal for most days of the year.

Anne was now thinner than in the past, and Nancy noticed that as her mother aged, she was more sensitive to changes in the temperature. Anne never did really adjust to forced-air heat or air-conditioning. She was always cold just before the furnace came on, and while she could still operate the thermostat, Nancy would occasionally come in and find it cranked up to 80° or higher, and then Anne was too warm. Air-conditioning posed similar problems. When Nancy discussed this with the heating contractor, he told her that many older persons complained of the same problem.

Gradually Nancy cleaned out Anne's closets, taking only those clothes that she knew her mother would never wear again. When Nancy told her mother that she was taking them to the poor, Anne tartly replied, "Then the poor will be very well dressed."

After Anne became bedfast, sweat shirts again came to the rescue. Because traditional gowns open down the front and are likely to bunch up and become uncomfortable under the body, Nancy came up with the idea of just splitting Anne's sweatshirts down the back, so that they became very warm, comfortable bedwear. Another simple solution.

"Everyone's Clothes Need Washing, Including Yours."

Personal hygiene is one of the stock stories of eldercare at any level. Kay was a frustrated daughter who could not persuade her 75-year-old mother Evelyn, still in her own house, to launder or dry-clean her clothing often enough. Having grown up in a poor family where scarce clothes had to be carefully conserved, Evelyn had reverted in her old age to thinking that washing or dry-cleaning her clothes would wear them out.

Even after Kay bought her mother a new washer and dryer, Evelyn simply could not get the hang of operating them. She complained that the controls were too complicated. Friends and family members were commenting on the hygiene issue, and Kay noticed that her mother was also bathing and using deodorant less often than she should. Gentle hints and even stronger suggestions did no good. Evelyn's clothes remained dirty, and both she and they began to smell.

Finally, her patience gone, Kay saw that stern measures were required. Arriving at Evelyn's house carrying a laundry basket and soap powder, she began gathering up clothes to wash. When Evelyn objected, Kay spoke firmly. "Everyone's clothes need washing, including yours. I won't debate this issue any longer. I'm laundering your clothes, and if you don't cooperate, I will ask our family doctor about placing you under psychiatric care."

Seeing that she would have to give in, Evelyn stopped resisting and even accepted instruction from Kay on how to operate the new machines. Toward the end of their laundry session, Kay told her mother that she would be glad to come over regularly once a week to help get her laundry done. Grudgingly, Evelyn accepted Kay's offer.

"I Am Here To Give You A Bath!"

All home-help agencies have a great deal of turnover. Clients frequently are sent different people on different shifts, with little or no notice, which can add to the confusion of an already bewildered, overwhelmed elder. Because agencies employ different people to perform different tasks, clients are often confronted with new faces every time they turn around.

When Diane's 85-year-old grandmother finally agreed to receive some help over and above the help family members could provide, Diane selected an agency and made the arrangements. The plan began well, with someone appearing on schedule to prepare meals and clean the house. And then an entirely different stranger arrived, announcing, "I am here to give you a bath!" Diane's grandmother summarily dismissed her, and that was the last time that the grandmother allowed anyone to come in and help. Can you blame her?

Agencies have employees for housekeeping, meal preparation, nursing, nurse's aide duties, and home health-care aides. A client who signs up for the full range of services may see as many as five different people during the course of a week. In my experience, the higher-paying the position, the more likely it is that the same individual will provide the same service the next time it is requested. On the other hand, the helpers who are most often needed are also the ones who change jobs most frequently and hence may not be available at the next call.

If you are considering hiring an agency, factor in the reality that you may face a revolving door full of people. How will this fly with the senior you are concerned about? How will you handle this situation yourself?

Does Gramps or Grannie Need A New Pair of Shoes?

Although we are beginning to hear about the older population's problems with alcohol and other drugs, we hear little about older folks gambling. Yet men and women who used to get up early to go to work now board planes or buses to be carried somewhere for a day or two of gambling. Gambling has become the second-biggest addiction in the country, and we now hear scientific reports of a gambling gene, like the gene that reportedly predisposes to the disease of alcoholism.

Today's retirees are more alone than in the past, because many of their friends are dead or have moved away, and their families may live far away or be too busy to make time for them. Gambling, especially riverboat gambling, is one of the fastest-growing forms of recreation for the elderly. Casinos beckon with free transportation, free food, a welcoming atmosphere, and the dream of immediate wealth. The gambling palaces offer a place to go, an opportunity to be "out among 'em," and a tremendously powerful lure. Thus a retiree who answers the call of the casinos may not be hard to understand.

With casino gambling now in more than half of the U.S. states, many older folks and retirees will become involved. Thousands already are. More than a quarter of those over 55 who were interviewed on this topic had gone to a casino to gamble at least once in the previous year. They often commented that they felt more accepted at casinos than at other places, even church. Sadly, many retirees feel marginalized and isolated in most aspects of their lives. In casinos, on the other hand, they are part of the mainstream.

What issues for families does gambling bring up? A huge one is the possibility for financial disaster. For adult children, the thought of a parent on a fixed income tripping off for a day of gambling is a frightening one. Yet many retirees simply shrug off their children's concern. Better to be short a few bucks at day's end, they figure, and have some pleasant memories, than spend day after day alone and bored to death.

Another issue gambling stirs up in the social one. Casino crowds include adults of both sexes and every age group. Many frequent players make no bones about the fact that going to a casino is a great way to meet potential mates — never mind that these prospects are equally dedicated to this risky new pastime. And unscrupulous persons may hang around casinos to prey on susceptible older folks. A few elderly gamblers talk about the highs they get from a little win, craving the excitement these trips bring to their otherwise mundane lives.

If you expect to look after your parent, is gambling likely to be a problem for either of you? If so, can you discuss it openly and frankly, seeking solutions before trouble occurs?

"Sex? Who? My Parents? My Grandparents? Perish The Thought!"

When was the last time you thought about your elders having sex? If most of us are honest, we think about it as little as possible. Yet now we are hearing of new drugs that help elderly people reclaim active sex lives. Millions are beating a path to their doctors to obtain prescriptions. Obviously, older folks are interested in prolonging or reclaiming their sexuality. Just because adult children are uncomfortable thinking about their parents' sex lives doesn't mean they don't want one.

For privacy's sake, elderly couples probably want to stay in their own homes as long as possible. If they must relocate, privacy may be an important issue. Adult children will have to deal with this matter more forthrightly than in the past. If such a person becomes yours to look after, who will fill Dad's or Uncle John's prescriptions for him? Who will take him to the doctor? Will there be issues around the laundering of the sheets, or about entertaining a visitor in private? Such questions must be faced and dealt with.

In the case of a man whose sexual vigor has been restored, there may be a woman in the background who is less than thrilled at the prospect. Some women believe that they and their partners have had an understanding, and then, suddenly, Granddad goes on the prowl. Women may worry about contracting sexually transmitted diseases from a wandering mate.

Occasionally a senile older man may make unwelcome approaches to those caring for him. Ginnie was embarrassed after her father began reaching out and grabbing some of the aides in the nursing home where he lived, asking them to come home with him or even to marry him. In his dementia, where sexual urges were concerned, he had lost all sense of decorum. Eventually the home's director asked Ginnie to meet with the nursing staff to explain that her father did not know what he was doing. She then gave the staff explicit instructions on how to respond to and defuse the unwelcome behavior.

In another household, Gramps began making unseemly remarks to a teenage granddaughter and on one occasion went so far as to fondle her breast. The girl did not know how to handle the sexual advances, and she was afraid to mention it to her parents, so thereafter she simply avoided her grandfather whenever possible and made sure that she was never in a room or in the house alone with him.

What issues might arise around sexual matters for the elderly persons in your life?

Self-Care

Caregivers may become so involved in caring for their elders that they neglect themselves. Self-care is extremely important. Most of us need help in examining how well we are caring for ourselves, and in looking at the various ways we can do it.

Chris was an only child who remembered how Irma, her mother, had brought her own mother into their home to look after her until she died. Chris tried to do the same for Irma, but after Irma had a massive stroke and became paralyzed on one side, Chris was unable to continue caring for her mother at home. Irma had to be turned in bed, lifted in and out of her wheelchair, and given heavy assistance in the bathroom. The rooms and halls in Chris's house were too small to accommodate these needs, and Chris herself was not physically strong enough to perform the tasks required in Irma's daily care.

Furthermore, Chris's husband Pete and their three growing children needed Chris's attention as well. So Chris arranged for Irma to spend several weeks in the physical rehabilitation unit where she herself held a flex-time position, hoping that the physical and occupational therapy would allow Irma to do more for herself. At the end of her course of therapy Irma was transferred to a nearby nursing home.

During this period, Chris put everyone else's needs ahead of her own. She worked conscientiously at her job. During breaks and lunch hour she visited her mother in the rehab unit. Then, after Irma was transferred, she stopped off every day after work at the nursing home, rushing home afterward to be with her children. She prepared two good meals for her family, day after day. She stopped taking her daily walks and started picking up fast-food snacks for lunch. She quit going to the hairdresser or paying any attention to her clothes. When she had a new driver's license photo taken, Chris was shocked at how old and worn-out she looked. Putting all her energies into caring for everyone else, she had stopped caring for herself.

A Self-Care Inventory

The following questions may help you decide how you are caring for yourself. Circle the answer that seems to fit your situation.

EXERCISE

3   I am sitting here sweating because I just got done for today.

2   I try to get out to walk several times a week.

1   How long ago was the Ice Age?

NUTRITION

3   I could be the American Heart Association poster child.

2   I watch my diet pretty carefully, but it could be improved.

1   Fast food is my thing. I just cannot get enough,

SUPPORT SYSTEM

3   I have lots of folks who matter to me, and I belong to several groups.

2   A few good friends, although I am not much for crowds.

1   I have always been a loner and spend little time making friends.

SPIRITUAL LIFE

3   Rich. I see many connections in the world and try to go with the flow.

2   Not a big deal. I go to church and try to live by the beliefs I have.

1   Nonexistent. I don't believe in anything that I can't see, touch, or taste. None of that religious malarkey for me.

MENTAL HEALTH

3   Good. I believe I know how to express a wide range of feelings.

2   Fair. I do question why things happen to me, and know that the range of feelings I can express is limited.

1   I cannot take much more of this. That's one reason I bought this book!

PHYSICAL WELL-BEING
3   Excellent. Rarely even have a cold.
2   OK. Don't have as much energy as in the past, but who does?
1   Not as good as it used to be. I wish I got around better, felt better.

SOCIAL ACTIVITIES
3   I went out earlier today. I am always on the go.
2   I went out a couple of days ago. I guess I have an active life.
1   It has been a while. Mostly I stay put, keep my own company.

WAKING UP
3   I always wake up r'aring to go.
2   A little sluggish, but once I am really awake, I can get moving.
1   Tired. I am tired almost all the time.

SLEEP
3   An airplane could land in the yard and I wouldn't wake up.
2   I sleep pretty well, wake up once or twice. Doesn't everyone?
1   Most of the time I sleep fitfully or not very well.

GENERAL OUTLOOK ON LIFE
3   Grateful and happy. Things come up, but I deal with them.
2   So-so. My outlook varies from day to day.
1   I feel sad much of the time, often dreading what the day may bring.

How many points did you accumulate? If your score was 20 or less, you may want to think about paying more attention to how you care for yourself.

"Nowadays I Can Hardly Put One Foot In Front Of The Other."

Nothing is more exhausting than ongoing, seemingly endless care for another person. One of the biggest issues caretakers face is exhaustion from all the responsibility. Are you feeling worn out with caring for an elderly relative or friend? Do you feel physically exhausted and emotionally drained?

If so, it is crucial to sort out whether you are just truly worn out or whether you may also be depressed. One of the surest signs of depression is disrupted sleep patterns. Someone who is merely tired can usually fall asleep and stay asleep all night, while a depressed person may fall asleep at first only to awaken one or several times throughout the night. Waking up very early in the morning is another possible sign of depression. Sleeping too much during the day is another.

Depressed persons often feel hopeless about their situation. They can see nothing positive in what is happening, and life becomes merely an endless series of obstacles to be overcome, with no light at the end of the tunnel.

Persons who are depressed may neglect their personal hygiene and grooming. Some eat too much, while others lose their appetites. Many depressed persons become sedentary, or at least far less active than in the past. Other suggestive symptoms include chronic neck or shoulder pain, chronic digestive difficulties, a tendency to cry easily, inability to experience joy, or shutting down all emotional response.

If any of these characteristics sound like you, or like the person you are caring for, it is time to consult a physician about the situation. A thorough physical examination is essential, along with an in-depth conversation with the doctor about the living situation. If the problem is indeed depression, remedies are available.

Just a little physical activity can often counteract depression and stimulate production of endorphins — substances naturally produced by the body that generate a feeling of well-being. A 10-minute walk, working out at a gym, or swimming three times a week at the Y — any of these can make a difference for the good.

Getting a massage can help enormously. So can relaxing for brief periods in a hot tub, especially if the tub has bubbling water jets. You may even want to purchase a moderately priced portable water bubbler to use in your bathtub at home. A class led by a qualified yoga teacher can make a huge difference. Many people find these gentle yoga workouts very relaxing and refreshing, and anyone can participate.

Having a broad enough support network is extremely important. The depressed caregiver is usually attempting to carry the whole burden alone, when the task is too much for any one person. If you cannot get out of the house to see people on a social basis, find other ways to keep up contacts. Can you talk on the phone to friends for brief periods each day? Do you have access to the Internet? Can you invite someone to your home for morning coffee, lunch, afternoon tea, a game of cards, or to watch a video? Daily contacts with others are very important for anyone in a caregiving role.

After looking after her semi-paralyzed mother for many months at home, Sylvia felt in desperate need of a break. Her solution was to call on her mother's much younger sister. This aunt had taken a nurse's aide course and was in good health herself and a competent caretaker. So Sylvia asked her to come and fill in, so that Sylvia and her husband could get away for a week. The mother's sister was happy to come. Sylvia and her husband benefitted greatly from their stay at the beach, while Sylvia's mother was likewise refreshed by having her sister with her instead of her overworked daughter.

"In The Light of Eternity, What Difference Does It Make?"

Whenever Don arranged to spend a little time with his aging mother, taking her out for lunch or supper, or for some other outing, she always wanted to carry a sweater along. Outdoors the temperature might be 100° with humidity to match, yet on leaving the house his mother invariably insisted on taking that sweater with her. Don felt annoyed and greatly frustrated, knowing that before the outing ended, he would have to carry the sweater and be responsible for it. He always tried to discourage his mother from taking it, and she always insisted. They went round and round and round on the sweater issue.

Then one day for some reason Don was able to see the thing differently. Realizing that the sweater was a boundary-and-control issue, he also remembered a favorite remark of his mother's, one he had heard her make many times when some decision had to be made. "In the light of eternity, what difference does it make?" In the case of the sweater, the answer was, no difference at all. Thereafter if his mother insisted on carrying the sweater, Don backed off and let her be.

A remark another wise parent made applies equally to child-care and eldercare. "Choose your battles." In other words, only make a big deal out of issues that really are big deals. For the rest, save your energy and let somebody else have his or her way. Another way of saying the same thing is, "Don't dull your pick on little rocks." If you wear yourself out fighting inconsequential battles, when the big issue comes up, both parties will already be worn out from conflict. Make things as easy on yourself as you can.

*   *   *

Here are a few questions to ponder.

What issues do you and your elder go round and round on? How important are they?
Is there a major issue around which you feel a strong need to be "right"? What is it?
Why do you think you are so attached to being right on this one?
In the light of eternity, what difference will your position make on this issue, or on others?

A Relaxing Root Canal

While her mother was alive, Brenda's life was so hectic that she wonders today how she ever sustained her marriage and teaching career while also attending to her mother's every need. Even with caregivers hired to be with her mother 24 hours a day, it was a major challenge.

During those last eight years, on an "average" day — a day without crises — Brenda got up early, made sure all was in readiness for her day's work, met her morning classes, ran over to her mother's apartment for a brief lunchtime visit, and returned to the campus for the afternoon's responsibilities. At the end of her working day she visited her mother's apartment again briefly, then headed home to her husband for the evening.

But many days were far from average. A caregiver might resign with no notice. Or her mother might need something overlooked in the general weekly shopping, such as the mountain of "blue pads" needed during the final year of her life. The last quart of milk might turn out to be sour, or the vacuum-cleaner bags might be all used up without anyone's noticing.

These unanticipated errands and staff changes caused the greatest chaos for Brenda. Once Brenda had planned to take an entire day off and was looking forward to it greatly — an entire day with nothing on the schedule. But by 9:00 a.m. everything had changed. The current caregiver fell ill herself, and Brenda had to locate the caregiver's own family to get her to the doctor, while Brenda's mother suddenly needed substitute care. By noon everything had been accomplished, but the anticipated free day was shot.

The following morning Brenda had a dental appointment. And as the dentist tipped back the chair to begin the first stages of her root canal, Brenda smiled, experiencing the most relaxing moment she had known in many days.

Some of us, particularly those who have played the Hero role in our dysfunctional families, frequently do more than is expected of us. We have a need to do things not just in a 100% way, but 200% or 300%. We may be workaholics, perfectionists, or both. And until we have had some guidance in looking at these patterns of behavior, we often leap in with immediate help when a little time and reflection might suggest alternative ways of handling a situation. Do you think these patterns apply to you?

If you were in a situation similar to Brenda's, what do you think you could do to make things better?

Would you feel constrained to visit your mother twice each day? Could you take care of unanticipated errands in other ways?

Many towns still have independent grocers and drugstores that deliver. Are there any in your town? Sometimes even a larger store will deliver, if asked. You won't know until you try.

Do you believe that all the things Brenda was suddenly called about were truly urgent needs? Is it possible that guilt, or fear of her mother's displeasure, may have impelled Brenda to make such an all-out effort on her mother's behalf?

This Will Not Last Forever

Whatever your situation may be at this moment, one thing is certain. It will change. Eventually everything changes. Today's situation will not last forever. Whatever you are involved with today is one day closer to being over than it was yesterday.

This, too, shall pass.

Whether you are dealing with a new realization that someone you love needs care, or facing moving that person or perhaps even yourself in order to take on the responsibility of the person's care, remember — it will not last forever.

If a change has taken place suddenly — a sudden illness or disability, or a death that changes everything — the shock waves of fear, anger, anxiety, or sadness will not last forever. If you have taken someone into your home, it will not last forever.

Whatever it is, it will pass. Nothing lasts forever.

Learning to take one day at a time can be a tremendous help. Sometimes taking things one hour or one minute at a time is as much as you can do. Just remember, however difficult the tasks may be that you are facing today, none of them will last forever.

This will not last forever.

A Dog, A Cat, Or Maybe Just A Goldfish

People talk more when dogs or cats are around, as therapists have discovered. Nowadays thousands of trained "therapy dogs" are regularly taken into hospitals and nursing homes around the country. Many families encourage elderly loved ones to adopt or purchase pets — and what a difference they make in so many lives.

Kathy noticed that John, her father, had stopped getting out much. He was lethargic and seemed mildly depressed. No physical explanation could be found, but it was clear to his wife, the extended family, and his doctor that he had lost his zest for life. Suddenly the solution occurred to Kathy — a dog!

She was able to find a relatively small, gentle, loving dog that immediately took to John and his wife. John began assuming responsibility for walking the dog, and soon he was getting out of the house several times a day. As he walked his dog, he often met people in the neighborhood who stopped to comment on his new friend, or ask questions about it. He found that he was pausing to visit with other dog-walkers, and sometimes they walked together, enjoying each other's company while giving their pets exercise. John's children soon noticed that he had a new topic of conversation, and his depression was gone.

In another town, when Dean's mother accepted a lovely cocker spaniel named Polly from a friend who had to go to a nursing home, pet and mistress were an immediate match. At first Polly was relegated to the sunroom, but soon her living quarters expanded, and one day while Dean was visiting, he caught Polly making herself comfortable on her mistress's bed. Now Polly and Dean's mom are nearly inseparable. They were instrumental in establishing a dog park in their area where pets can frolic and owners sit and visit. When they are apart, it's impossible to say which one misses the other more.

If you are considering bringing an older person into your home but must go out every day to work yourself, a small pet may provide companionship while you are away. Of course this will work only if the elderly person is able to get about and not likely to be upset by the presence of the pet. An older person who lives alone may also welcome an animal to relieve that loneliness.

Although people often comment that dogs are "more work" than cats, dogs also have ways of comforting people that are quite humanlike. Our dog Spicey often sat by my mother's favorite chair in the afternoon during our visits, and my mother viewed our dog as her dog. She even once told me she was beginning to prefer Spicey to her grandchildren — my brother's children, who lived far away. When I asked why, she said simply, "Well, I see more of her than I do of them."

On the day my mother died, Spicey sat close to us throughout the morning at my mother's apartment. Occasionally I would pick her up and hold her for a bit on my lap, or she might rest her head and front paws on my mother's bed. It was a quiet, peaceful time. After Mother died, when the funeral director came for her body, Spicey and I rode along in the hearse, Spicey again resting her head and paws on my mother's body. When it was time to bury my mother Spicey went with us too, and after the casket was in the ground, we set her down so that she could walk around, as if to inspect the site. Then she seemed at peace.

A Son Can Do It Well

The bond between Richard and his mother was a very strong one. Richard's father, a compulsive gambler, had deserted the family when Richard was two years old, and Richard's mother had had to bring up Richard and his older brother and sister by herself. Fortunately, a grandmother and aunt who lived nearby were willing to help, but Richard knew that his mother had always had a struggle and respected her for her hard work and success.

Although daughters are usually the ones who end up caring for their elderly parents or other relatives, in this case Richard wanted to do it. He lived alone, and he could never forget everything his mother had done for him. Now he wanted to do the best he could for her.

The two of them — mother and son — had always had a special bond. Few words were exchanged between them, but they understood one another, respected one another, and had no taboo subjects between them. Richard intended to be there for his mother whenever she needed him, and she knew that that was so.

When the time came that his mother required daily care, Richard brought her into his own home and arranged for caregivers during the day while he was at work. Because his mother was having difficulty adjusting to the medications prescribed for her, she was often sick at her stomach. As Thanksgiving approached, she did not feel like joining in a big celebration, so she and Richard spent the holiday together in Richard's home. That Thanksgiving — a day when families usually sit down to a great feast — Richard's mother was persistently sick at her stomach, and Richard had placed a plastic bucket beside the bed in case of need.

His mother indicated that she was about to be sick again, and as Richard picked up the bucket and held it for her, she said, "Oh, Richard, I am so sorry to do this to you."

"It's OK, Mom. You're sick, that's all," he said. "You don't have to apologize to me."

But his mother continued to say how sorry she was, how bad she felt about needing his help. Finally Richard said, "Mom, you took care of me when I had nonstop diarrhea as a kid, until the doctor discovered I was allergic to milk. That went on for weeks and weeks."

"That was a privilege," she replied.

"Taking care of you is my privilege," Richard responded.

After that Richard's mother's health continued to decline until she finally became confined to bed. One Saturday afternoon Richard was sitting beside her talking, when his mother suddenly touched her fingers to his cheek. "I see God right here," she said. With tears filling his eyes, Richard knew that caring for his mother was one of the greatest privileges he could have. It was worth all the effort required.

"When My Mom Got Better, I Wanted To Kill Her!"

The last three years of Ellen's mother's life were extremely trying. Every year, on the anniversary of Ellen's father's death, her mother went into a decline, staying in bed, seldom eating, taking few fluids, and sleeping almost around the clock. Each year the same pattern returned, although each time after several weeks her mother would gradually improve.

Even after Ellen's mother became demented, unable to produce a coherent sentence or, at times, speak at all, the cycle continued to repeat itself. Ellen concluded that at a very deep level her mother somehow "knew" the time of the year and was trying to let go in order to join her departed husband.

Ellen and her mother had long since mended the difficult relationship that had previously existed between them. Before her decline became severe, Ellen's mother had actually become able to nurture and support Ellen in ways that Ellen had always longed for but never before known. Both women were grateful for the change.

Mother and daughter had become each other's protectors, to whatever degree was possible. Ellen's mother did anything she could to help Ellen, and Ellen became fiercely protective of her mother's dignity, memories, wishes, home, material possessions, and reputation. Ellen's feelings toward her mother were truly bittersweet — gratitude that the relationship had changed so much for the better, mingled with deep regrets that it had been so long in coming.

But as her mother went steadily downhill, in the midst of one of these withdrawal cycles, Ellen knew that she herself had grown very tired. Believing that her mother had finished her work on this earth, Ellen became completely ready to let her go.

And then, amazingly, once again her mother began to rally. Ellen felt more frustrated than she had ever felt before. She had had enough! She wanted to get on with her own productive life, and her frustration was such that she actually had the thought, "It's time for my mother to die. If she doesn't die, I feel as if I could kill her."

Knowing she could never carry out such an act and shocked at even harboring the thought, Ellen phoned a friend who had gone through an equally distressing long-term illness with a family member. After she told him what was going on, his answer was a single word: "Yes!" He understood, because he had had exactly the same thought. "Of course, Ellen, you would never do such a thing, I know," he said, "but yes, you do reach such a point. Don't worry about it. It's reality, and it's OK."

Ellen felt liberated, and her frustration dissipated, never again to reach such a high level. She began to see her mother's strength in a new light and realized again, for the umpteenth time, that only God knew her mother's timeline, and that her mother's work on this earth was not yet done, because she was still providing Ellen with lessons to be learned.

Different Strokes For Different Folks, and How To Get What You Need

Becky's mother Marie was close to death. She had an impacted bowel, and the doctor had made a house call to deal with it. (Lucky family, to have a doctor who makes house calls!) Although by then Marie was barely capable of speech, she turned to Becky at that moment and said distinctly, "No more." She was making it clear that she wanted to be allowed to die. Becky told the doctor she would respect her mother's wishes, asking him to give her mother only comfort care from that point on.

But Marie's caregivers bristled at this change in the treatment approach. Surprised by their attitude, Becky asked them to join her in an early-morning meeting that could include the night and the day shifts. One caregiver told how an uncle of hers had had the same problem and was cured by surgery, and she thought Becky should do the same for Marie. When Becky asked how old her uncle was and what other medical problems he had had, the caregiver replied that he was in his 50s and had no other problems. Becky then stated that she thought her mother's situation was quite different; she was 83, with severe dementia, and had made it clear to Becky that when the time came, she wanted simply to be let go.

Becky went on to say that for as long as she could remember, her Christian upbringing had emphasized the belief that all persons come from God, belong to God, and are going back to God. For Becky, this message made it much easier to anticipate and face her mother's death.

Nevertheless, some caregivers held precisely the opposite view. In order to stave off death, they were determined to do everything possible for as long as possible. They clearly saw themselves as waging a life-and-death combat, no matter how debilitated or how ready to go Marie might be. That day Becky came to see that death issues are really "where the rubber hits the road."

Other conflictual issues also came out in that meeting. One of the caregivers complained that Becky was running everything. Becky responded that she knew her mother's views and intended to honor them. Finally all agreed that any caregiver unable to view death as a welcome release for Marie, who was worn out from the struggle, would be better employed with some other family, and Becky would understand and replace the person as soon as she was able.

Boundary issues and power issues are very often points of conflict in such situations. Fortunately, Becky's convictions were strong enough to see her and her mother through.

A *"Bed & Breakfast"*

Fatigue is inevitable for the caregiver of a person with long-term chronic illness or progressive debility. The unrelenting responsibility, not the work, is what gets to so many of us. Yet creative solutions can certainly be found.

Lori, a forward-thinking woman in the Midwest who understands that caregivers sometimes need a break, operates an establishment rather like a Bed & Breakfast, where elderly persons can receive round-the-clock care for up to two weeks at a time. Housed in a Victorian dwelling that naturally lends itself to accommodation for 8-10 individuals, this "B&B" has no stereotypical institutional features. The atmosphere is homelike, and aides are available to help clients get out and do things compatible with their abilities. Three appealing, nutritious meals are part of the daily package.

Sound like heaven? It probably is for both the guests and their regular caregivers. Family members can avail themselves of the service to get a much-needed rest, and hired caregivers can have time off for vacation, family occasions, and the like.

*   *   *

Could such a facility be set up in your area? The questions below may help you come up with a creative solution of your own.

What respite facilities does your area already have?
How do individuals qualify for these facilities?
What are the charges for respite care?
What do you think the market for respite care is in your area?
Are there any vacant or moderately priced houses in areas already zoned for such a facility?
How many people do you know who might be interested in going in with you to create such a facility?
What other ways can you think of to gather together a group of caregivers who might be interested in such a venture?
What might stop you or hold you back?
What funding might be available from your community, state, or others to get you going?

"Good Care, Poor Care — Who Cares?"

Many families are discovering lately that the quality of care their elders receive in doctors' offices or hospital emergency rooms is not as good as it once was.

Barbara will never forget an afternoon spent in the E.R. with her 75-year-old mother. Roberta had fallen in the beauty shop, and after she had difficulty getting up, the shop owner felt that she should go to the E.R., so Barbara was called to take her. Once there, minutes turned into hours. When Barbara complained, she was told that the E.R. personnel were extremely busy, although several staffers were sitting at the desk, one reading a magazine. Roberta was finally examined and sent home with no treatment.

A week later, Roberta fell again, and this time Barbara wanted to know why. In the E.R. again, Roberta was found to have a broken hip, and the doctor speculated that she had broken it in the first fall. Barbara asked to have her mother hospitalized for additional tests. The doctor replied that insurance companies, not doctors, made such decisions nowadays. Holding her ground about wanting her mother hospitalized, Barbara was then told that no beds were available.

As her frustration grew, Barbara spotted one of Roberta's friends from the hospital nursing staff. Within seconds after Barbara told her what was going on, Roberta was admitted. The irony was that Roberta was the retired Chief of Nursing Education for that particular state. She had spent her professional life working to improve hospital care, yet as an elderly person she could not even gain admission to a hospital without someone pulling strings.

Recent news articles confirm this distressing trend. One reported the shocking results of a study of 13,000 nursing homes in a five-state area. To sum up, the oldest cancer patients in nursing homes often received no pain medication whatsoever — not even aspirin. Minority patients were found to receive less care than white patients. The trends regarding the elderly were clear. The older the patients, the less pain medication they received.

Health-maintenance organization (HMO) cutbacks in care for the elderly also raise grave concerns for patients and their families. Laura, an 84-year-old woman suffering from unrelenting vaginal bleeding, had great difficulty just getting an appointment with her doctor. Relatives' efforts to help made little difference. When she finally was seen, the doctor diagnosed uterine cancer, saying Laura needed surgery as soon as possible. Yet a second doctor said she should never have the operation. What is best for Laura? How can she and her family know? Does her age make a difference in the decision? Which is the better treatment? In such cases, families are caught in a horrible dilemma.

Clearly, elderly persons need someone, or a combination of someones, to advocate for them. Yet even with advocates there may be a tendency to provide minimal care — to send elderly patients on their way without finding out what is wrong with them or intervening to help them get well.

*   *   *

You may find it helpful to answer these questions about your elderly relative's medical care.

What is the person's overall state of health?
When was the last time she (or he) was seen by a physician or
    nurse practitioner?
Beyond Medicare or Medicaid, what medical coverage does the
    person have?
When was the last medical crisis?
How was it resolved?
Who is available to take or go with the person to the doctor?
What do you believe are the doctor's policies in treating this
    person?
What do you believe are the hospital's policies for treating the
    elderly?
Does your local hospital have a Quality Control Committee?
What plan do you intend to follow if care is needed for this
    person?
Who might be the patient's advocate(s)?

Elder Abuse: An Elephant In The Living Room

"An elephant in the living room" is any major situation that everyone in the family knows about, but no one talks about. Regrettably, elder abuse can be such an "elephant." News media occasionally report an elderly person found suffering from mal-nutrition, bruises, burns, or broken bones. Some abused elders are capable of describing what happened, while others are unable or unwilling to do so. In every such case, however, the abused person has been dependent upon someone who, for whatever reason, failed to care for the person with patience, compassion, and love.

Why do such things happen? Unresolved parent-child issues, caregiver stress, mental-health problems (on either side or both), alcoholism or other-drug addiction, and isolation are just a few of the causes. If the older person was abusive when the child was young, the now-adult caregiver may seize this opportunity to "pay the parent back." Painful unresolved family issues between parent and child thus can have grave consequences many decades after the original events. Even a caregiver who does not intend to behave uncaringly may simply "crack" under conditions of unrelenting stress and isolation, and then the abuse just happens.

Ted's mother had died young, of tuberculosis. After her death, Ted's womanizing father, George, took no further interest in his children's well-being, becoming an alcoholic tramp. George never strayed far from the community where he and his wife had grown up and other relatives lived, but his children soon had to be placed in an orphanage. For years George drunkenly wandered the countryside, sleeping in barns or out in the woods.

Ted, an intelligent boy, graduated from high school, obtained a college scholarship, and was able with a benefactor's help to go on to medical school. He married an attractive nurse, went into partnership practice in a distant town, and seemed to be functioning well in every way. But as George aged and his alcoholism took its toll on his health, he found out where Ted lived and showed up wheedling Ted to take him into his home. Ted was angry about his father's abandonment of his family, embarrassed at having him show up on his doorstep as a dis-reputable tramp, and fearful of the impact on his very fine reputation in the community.

In short, Ted refused to take on his father's care. Briefly debating what his duty might be, he quickly recognized that his resentment toward his father was so great that he could not care for him in a compassionate way. Ted's solution to his dilemma was to arrange with the county welfare department to take on his father's case, wisely acknowledging that that was as far as he was emotionally able to go.

Some people are just plain mean. If you face the need to care for someone who was or is still abusive of you, the best guarantee for a successful outcome is to recognize any issues still operative in the relationship, do your best to work through them, possibly with professional help from a counselor or minister, and continue striving to avoid isolation and reduce stress in your day-to-day situation. All easier said than done, but vitally important nevertheless. Many communities and some hospitals have support groups for those caring for elderly relatives or friends. Discussing your experiences with others who understand can be a big help.

Getting The Secrets Out, Moving Beyond The Fear

"We are only as sick as our secrets," you may sometimes hear, if you take part in any mutual-help or therapeutic group. Secrecy and fear operate in every case of elder abuse, just as in every case of child abuse. The elderly person may not talk about what is happening for fear of more abuse, neglect, abandonment, or institutional placement. And the abusive caregiver certainly will not speak of it, for fear of criminal prosecution.

In some situations, the elderly person may be the dangerous one. Disoriented or irrational elderly people have been known to set fires, on purpose or accidentally, or create other danger-ous situations if they are not adequately supervised. For Cheryl, her husband Jim, and their teenage children, life became unbearable when Cheryl's mother who had been living with them became demented. She would slip out of the house at all hours of the day or night, until Cheryl was truly afraid even to go to sleep. This disturbed grandmother suffered under the delusion that Cheryl's children were actually her children and would fly into a rage whenever Cheryl attempted to discipline them. A family whose day-to-day life is being turned nightmarish by the presence of a disturbed older person in the house needs and deserves support to weather the situation with good grace.

Fortunately, hotlines are being set up nationwide so that concerned persons may report potential elder abuse, and families in turmoil can ask for help. State laws are changing, with many states setting up teams to work county by county with families where abuse or neglect is suspected. Your local Department of Social Services is usually a good place to begin looking for such assistance.

Rather than attacking the suspected abuser, these teams make every effort to support all those caught in the stressful situation. They seek to empower the elderly person, making it clear that nothing will be allowed to happen that the senior does not want to happen. They share with the caregivers information about resources for help with housekeeping, personal care, meals prepared in or delivered to the home, adult day care, counseling, emergency housing, and financial or legal assistance. When the secret is no longer a secret, solutions can be found in most cases that do not call for removing the elderly person from the home.

"I'll Tell You A Secret . . . "

Janet's mother, Florence, had a secret. Her secret was that her father and mother had never been married. Florence was almost 75 years old before she learned who her father was. It had never been talked about in her family, and her mother had eventually married a man with whom she had three sons. Yet Florence kept her mother's maiden name, and her mother never discussed her father with her, or, as far as Florence knew, with anyone else.

Florence's secret — her illegitimacy — dominated her life. Early on, she adopted the notion that she had to be perfect, and that relentless drive for perfection led to a whiz-bang career, even though she left home at 17 with just $10 that she had borrowed from an uncle. Keeping her secret also created a powerful need for control that affected all her future relationships.

After Florence finally learned from a cousin who her father was, she knew all that she wanted to know. He had actually married into the family and had always been "around" as she grew up. He had known where she was and who she was, yet he made no effort to get to know her, much less to be part of her life. Therefore she wanted nothing to do with him. And yet that secret dominated her life.

After Florence died, it dawned on her daughter Janet that Florence's father was also her grandfather. Funny how that fact had escaped her for most of her life! She decided to try to find him, which turned out to be fairly easy. She started with the census listings, found his death certificate in the county records, his obituary in an old issue of the local paper, and his grave marker in the cemetery.

Locating his son — her uncle — and grandchildren in the telephone book, Janet wrote and then called, and shortly thereafter she was given two photographs of her grandfather and a little information about the kind of person he was. In the photographs Janet saw remarkable resemblances between her grandfather and mother. Their skin, their hands, their mouths, and even the way they held their right hands — startlingly identical.

Janet and her uncle have since been blessed with an ever-deepening friendship and connection. This same uncle and his wife have a great-granddaughter who lives with them most of the time. When this child realized that her last name is not the same as her sisters', Janet and her aunt and uncle saw family history repeating itself in this beautiful little girl. Now they focus on helping her to be free of the secrecy and emotional defenses that Florence took on in order to cope with her life situation. They talk with her, answer her questions to the best of their ability, and have let her know that they will help her find her father if and when she chooses to do so. They want no more family secrets. They do not want this history to repeat itself again.

When families keep secrets, those secrets do repeat themselves. People are frequently astounded when they realize how often it happens. The result of keeping secrets is negative in too many ways. For everyone's well-being, secrets need to be given up.

※   ※   ※

You may want to consider these questions to see if any secrets are lurking in your family.

Did anyone commit suicide?
Have there been any illegitimate births?
Has anyone declared bankruptcy?
Has anyone served time in prison?
What about alcoholism or other-drug addiction?
Are there family members who are just not talked about?
Have any relatives dropped out of the picture — perhaps just
    disappeared?
How many divorces have there been?
What about sudden unexplained deaths?
Any evidence or suggestion of physical or sexual abuse?
Have there been any unexplained "blank" periods of time —
    family history that remains unaccounted for?
Does anything else come to mind?

The truth will set you free.

A Jam Sandwich

Carole felt like a jam sandwich — jammed between two tremendous stressors in her life. Her mother, whom Carole had always perceived as distant and difficult, had suffered a calamitous stroke and had to be moved to a nursing home in her town to be looked after, while Carole's 16-year-old son was causing tremendous turmoil because of his growing love affair with alcohol, marijuana, and other drugs. Carole knew that he was using these substances, but she didn't know what to do about it, and neither did her addiction-ignorant husband, even though he was a busy physician.

Carole dragged herself through the days wondering if this torture would ever cease. Every weekend brought new crises where her son was concerned, and weekdays were a weary round of going to work, checking on her mother, and dragging back home to look after her family. A major element in her depression was the guilt she felt about having a son whose behavior was such a disgrace. She blamed herself as a bad parent, although eventually she would learn from family recovery support groups that none of the fault lay with her. Perhaps her greatest dread was that her mother would find out about this wayward son and think less of Carole for it.

Visiting her mother in the nursing home one Sunday afternoon, Carole noticed that her mother seemed more lucid than usual, more approachable. Since the stroke her mother's disposition had softened a great deal. On impulse, Carole found the courage to say, "Mother, I'd like you to know about something I've been going through. Maybe you can say some prayers for me and my family about it."

"What is it?" her mother asked, concern showing in her eyes.

"It's Joe," Carole said. "He's 16 now, and we've been having a great deal of trouble with him, drinking, smoking marijuana, getting in trouble with the law. We don't know what to do about it. So if I seem down in the dumps sometimes, that's probably the reason."

Her mother stretched out a soft hand from under the cover and patted Carole's hand where it lay on the bed. When Carole raised her eyes to her mother's face, she saw tears glistening in her mother's eyes. "Oh, darling, I wish so much that you didn't have to go through this. I will pray about it, and maybe he will come to his senses soon."

Sharing her burden frankly with her mother and receiving the degree of comfort, however feeble, that her mother was able to offer gave Carole a lift that she remembered for many days. She recalled then that in years gone by, her mother, who had been chronically depressed, had often tried to offer encouragement to friends who were struggling with alcoholism or depression in their own families. She had even helped to get several men, including a nephew, into Alcoholics Anonymous. Carole realized that her mother understood more than she had given her credit for and felt a burden lifted just by sharing her problem with her parent.

A Person She Had Never Known, A Relationship That Had Never Been

Over the years Sara had devised various explanations for her tense relationship with her mother. Early on, her mother had been a busy career woman with little time for her child. Later, in adolescence and young adulthood, Sara had made a strong, healthy attempt to separate from her mother emotionally. By the time she went away to college, she viewed the home she returned to in the summers as her parents' home, but not hers.

After she and Bob married, Sara noticed that whenever she and her mother were together, they got along well for a few hours, perhaps even a whole day, but then their conflicts surfaced again and the relationship turned sour. The time came, finally, when Sara had to move her widowed mother to the town where she and Bob lived. New hopes arose. Perhaps if both of them were in the same town, Sara reasoned, she could watch over her mother while going on with her own life. They would finally have time to work things out.

In one way Sara was right, yet in another she was sadly mistaken. She had never imagined that from the moment her mother moved into her new place, she would become completely dependent upon her daughter. Sara was shocked and greatly frustrated by this new state of affairs. Having always seen her mother as a very strong woman, she had imagined that, settled in her new situation, her mother would involve herself in activities, make friends (she already had two friends of long standing in the same apartment building), and once again bloom where she was planted.

It didn't happen. In fact, Sara suddenly found herself saddled with a person she had never known — an utterly dependent mother. She tried everything. She introduced her mother to her friends. She took her to the public library and got her started checking out books. She phoned the minister of a church within walking distance of her mother's apartment, asking him to visit her mother and invite her to participate in church life. Nothing came of any of these efforts.

Meanwhile, Sara was coming to terms with her own drinking problem. Finally admitting her need for help, she began attending A.A. and seeing an addiction counselor. Knowing that sobriety was all-important in her life, she was nevertheless being pulled apart by her mother's insecurity demands. Sara needed to keep her counseling appointments and make all her meetings, yet her mother seemed to want Sara by her side 24 hours a day.

As Sara struggled to care for herself in new ways, her mother became more isolated, also drinking, and her demands on Sara became relentless. Nothing worked out as Sara had hoped. Instead of the lovely unfolding of a true mother-daughter relationship, Sara once again felt herself at the mercy of her mother — a different mother whose dependency controlled the relationship, just as her strength had controlled it in the past.

Sara felt trapped, wishing that she had never moved her mother to her town. After the final phone call in a long series of calls on one particular day, Sara found herself screaming into the phone: "You didn't take care of me when I was a child, and I am not taking care of you now!"

Desperate, Sara phoned her sister in a distant state, and together they decided that the only way out was to hire people to assume some of the duties that their mother was trying to force on Sara. The sister promised financial help if needed. Mother resisted; Sara and her sister persisted. To a degree, the plan worked. After someone was hired to help Sara's mother with errands and daily chores, Sara was then able to spend time with her mother in new ways. Her parent's basic needs were being met, Sara was available to help out in any emergency, and the two of them began to heal their relationship.

Why were they able to do this? First, because, in recovery, Sara was discovering some coping skills that helped her to detach from her mother in healthy ways. Her mother began to lose her grip on her daughter. Sara became more able to tolerate her mother without feeling frustrated, guilty, or both. As she learned more about the usual progression of relationships in families where there was alcoholism, she came to see that her situation was not an unusual one.

Finally Sara was also able to arrange a mini-intervention for her mother, with the help of her own addictions counselor, her mother's doctor, and Sara's sister. Once their mother stopped drinking, life changed very much for the better. Her memory cleared somewhat, and after she got over her anger about no longer being able to drink, she seemed a bit happier overall. Mother and daughter were then able to talk on a level different from any they had known before. Recovery made that possible.

Eventually, they were able to talk about almost everything. Sara's mother revealed a family scandal affecting her that Sara had never known about, which helped Sara to understand some of her mother's old behaviors. Thereafter Sara was able to grieve the loss of the affectionate childhood that she had never had and could forgive her mother. And once forgiveness had happened, they could talk about anything and everything.

In the end, Sara's mother became one of the best friends she ever had. She still misses her mother and probably always will.

Helping A Parent To Say Goodbye

Pauline had two children — Aaron and Linda. Aaron lived on the West Coast, while Linda lived in the Northeast. And when the time came that Pauline could no longer live alone in her big-city apartment, Linda helped her to move into a nice condominium close to her own suburban home. Linda willingly took on the responsibility of seeing that her mother had everything she needed, and things seemed to work out fairly well. Aaron contributed financial support, while Linda saw to the day-to-day needs.

Eventually, however, after Pauline suffered the first of several heart attacks, Linda had to bring her into her own home and arrange for nursing care. As Pauline lost more and more ground, physically and mentally, she sometimes asked for Aaron. Linda had always joked that Pauline loved her son more than her daughter. To Linda, it was not a big deal. She knew that their mother loved them both.

During one of Pauline's especially low times, when she asked for Aaron again, Linda phoned him, and he flew in from California. Arriving late at night, Aaron followed Linda into their mother's room, and although Pauline awakened, Aaron merely kissed his mother, told her he would see her in the morning, and tiptoed out again.

Next morning Linda got up early to help her mother bathe and dress. Pauline pointed to her new, peach-colored bathrobe, indicating that she wanted to put it on and sit up in a living-room chair. Linda helped her to do all this, and although Pauline had not spoken a clear sentence for weeks, Linda continued speaking to her as she always did, as if she could understand everything. Once Pauline was settled in the chair, Linda knelt down in front of her and said, "Mother, Aaron is here."

Pauline looked directly at her and said firmly and clearly, "I know that Aaron is here."

When Aaron entered the room, Pauline seemed transformed. No longer was she that frail, bedridden, deranged woman, a shadow of her former self, who muttered "Sooty, pooty, mooty," or occasionally let go with a "Whooooo" out of the blue. She was herself, only humbler and more accessible, in a stately way. The entire day she was like that, and it was a very special, quiet time. The door to the terrace was open, and a little breeze came in. For most of the day Pauline and her two adult children just sat together quietly and companionably, feeling little need to speak.

Toward late afternoon Aaron began to prepare to return to the airport. As he went over to tell his mother goodbye, Pauline reached out, grasped his hand with her thin one, looked up at him, and said, "I want you always to remember me." And Aaron said, "You don't have to worry, Mom. I always will."

Not long afterward, Pauline died, quietly and peacefully. Linda and Aaron were both grateful for the special time they had had with their mother before she was gone — time to be there as she summoned whatever strength she found within her to say that last goodbye. It was a humbling, moving experience, an experience filled with love and awe.

Reprinted here are portions of a speech delivered decades ago by my mother, Louise A. Meyer, R.N., a professional nursing educator. The reader will see that she anticipated many of the difficulties and potential solutions relative to health care for our aging population today.

AGING
A Nurse's Views

I believe . . . . that society in general does not willingly care for its older citizens . . . . Nurses, like other professional groups, have made very little effort to prepare their members to meet the needs of the aged . . . .

Aging is a process which begins with conception and ends with death, although we commonly think of aging as taking place after middle age. Aged, however, means old; it connotes that one has arrived at the state when certain characteristic results of the aging process have appeared . . . . Age is more a matter of physical and mental aging than it is of chronologic processes. Tremendous variations exist; some people are physically and mentally old at thirty-five, while others are young at sixty-five . . . .

Although tremendous headway has been made . . . . in increasing life expectancy, relatively little progress has been made in the control and treatment of chronic diseases occurring in old age . . . . Kathleen Newton, in her book . . . . *Geriatric Nursing* . . . . insists that the phrase "the problem of the aged" should appear less often in our future thinking and writing and urges that we concentrate more on the satisfactions of old age, which can be many . . . .

There is a need for a change in attitude toward the aged . . . . It is seldom that we find a nurse who really enjoys working with the aged . . . . nurses, like other people, tend to shrink from the reminder that our hair shall become gray, our joints knuckled, our voices cracked, and our place in society less valued . . . . We find that the aged are less wanted than the young . . . .

The needs of the aged are identical with those of very young or people at any other stage of life: recognition, novelty of experience, security, and love . . . . Careful preparation for and practice in the care of the aged, with special emphasis on the satisfactions to be obtained in working with older people, should be a definite part of every nurse's preparation . . . .

The first objective in trying to meet the nursing problem is to keep the aged out of hospitals and nursing homes . . . . Public-health nurses and others concerned with the patient at home should do everything possible to keep the aged person at home as long as possible, since the aged usually would much rather be at home than anywhere else. Nursing problems increase when a patient is in strange surroundings and must learn new routines.

The aged need to be purposefully busy just as any other age group — this applies whether a person is at home, in a nursing home or other institution . . . . The aged . . . . sometimes have skills that are relatively unknown to younger generations and feel very proud when they are called upon to teach their particular skill to someone else. We are often wise to urge full or part-time employment as long as an aged person can do the work and is happy doing it, to furnish a purpose, sense of belonging, etc.

The aged need someone to care — and that someone may have to come from a group such as this [nursing professionals], since old people often outlive their close relatives and friends. Nursing care for the aged should demonstrate such qualifications as sympathetic kindliness and thoughtfulness without pity; sense of humor; tolerance, patience and tact, for the aged occasionally appear unreasonable. It is also important that caregivers maintain flexibility, since older people may appear fixed in their ways, and needless adherence to procedure achieves nothing and makes them unhappy. Friendliness, warmth, and genuine interest in people are also important, because the aged are often lonely and alone. The ability to manage the patient without appearing to manage him is also essential.

The nurse also has teaching responsibilities with the aged patient. This requires an attitude of optimism which will cause the nurse to regard the patient as though he were going to go on living for a very long time. The nurse will then give the aged patient the benefit of her knowledge and experience in teaching him and his relatives how to live with his illness, helping them to formulate their questions for the doctor, how to avoid problems, and how to meet problems when they occur. . . .

The nurse also has an important role in the rehabilitation of the patient. Many of the chronic illnesses of older people cannot be cured, according to our current medical knowledge. But many can be controlled in part, and what is more important, the person can be taught to live with his disease and can often be fitted into another area of employment so that his age or chronic illness may not too greatly lessen his earning capacity. Sometimes this may mean learning a new vocation, and our attitudes about this must be revisited. Many are inclined to think that the older person cannot learn a new trade . . . . Rehabilitation of the chronically ill aged person will often make employment possible and may enable the person to live fairly happily and still contribute to society . . . .

From the standpoint of cost alone, it is much cheaper to encourage rehabilitation of every possible person, and we urge nurses to accept their full responsibility for the rehabilitation of the aged . . . .

In summary, nursing care should be characterized by regularity in management, wherever the older person is, for he gains security from a fixed schedule and meets change with difficulty. He appreciates knowing what is coming next. Patients need to be encouraged in self-care and urged to help others if they are able to do so.

As much ambulation or movement should be encouraged as the patient can tolerate without fatigue. No patient should be kept in bed who can sit up, or be allowed to sit if he can walk. It is important to recognize that the aged move and think at a slower tempo. All treatment must be gentle and overtreatment avoided. The dosage of drugs is usually reduced and sedatives avoided wherever possible. Regular toileting should be practiced. Special attention must be given to nutritional needs. There is some indication that the senile patient has special dietary requirements.

It is highly desirable to keep the older person at home as long as possible, but when he must be institutionalized, the nursing home or hospital should approximate the community life from which the patient came, as nearly as possible. Every patient who is capable of it should have a job to perform. No matter how simple the task, he should realize that everyone is dependent upon him to do it.

And, since the aged person often feels that he has outlived his usefulness, that there is nothing left that is important in life for him to do, and that people don't want him — it is particularly important that the nursing care of the aged be concerned with personal relationships. Reassurance, kindness, and fostering of companionship can be cultivated to bring love and warmth into the important relationships. At the same time, the aged patient should not be overprotected to the point of becoming infantile, but should be encouraged to develop as much independence as the patient can assume.

RESOURCE LIST

ORGANIZATIONS

Alzheimer's Association
919 N. Michigan Avenue, Suite 1000
Chicago, IL 60611
1-800-272-3900

Alzheimer's Disease Education and Referral Center
    of the National Institute on Aging
1-800-438-4380

Children of Alcoholics Foundation
33 West 60th Street, 5th Floor
New York, NY 10023
1-800-359-2623

National Council on Alcoholism and Drug Dependence
1-800-NCA-CALL

National Family Caregivers Association
1-800-272-3900

WEBSITES

Alzheimers.com

The Alzheimer Page
www.biostat.wusti.edu/alzheimer

National Family Caregivers Association
www.nfacares.org

National Institute of Mental Health
www.nimh.nih.gov

National Depressive and Manic Depressive Association
www.ndmda.org

National Alliance for the Mentally Ill
www.nnami.org

BOOKS

Albom, Mitch. *Tuesdays With Morrie.* Doubleday. 1997.

Carter, J. *The Virtues of Aging.* Ballantine. 1998.

Cheever, S. *Home Before Dark.* Houghton Mifflin. 1984.

Cohen, D., & Eisdorfer, C. *The Loss of Self.* Plume. 1986.

Cox, L. *Dear Dad.* Saybrook. 1987.

Hargrave, T.D. & Anderson, W.T. *Finishing Well.* Brunner/Mazel. 1992.

Howard, J. *Families.* Simon & Schuster. 1978.

Jacobs, R. *Be An Outrageous Older Woman.* Harper Collins. 1997.

Johnson, V. *Intervention: How To Help Someone Who Doesn't Want Help.* Harper & Row. 1987.

L'Engle, M. *Summer of the Great Grandmother.* Harper San Francisco. 1996.

Lester, A., & Lester, J. *Understanding Aging Parents.* Westminster. 1980.

McGurn, S. *Under One Roof.* Parkside. 1992.

Mace, N., and Rabins, P. *The 36-Hour Day.* Johns Hopkins. 1981.

Maclay, E. *Green Winter.* Holt. 1990.

Moynahan, M. *Parting Is All We Know of Heaven.* Harper & Row. 1990.

Pipher, M. *The Shelter of Each Other.* Ballantine. 1996.

Powell, L., & Courtice, K. *Alzheimer's Disease.* Addison-Wesley. 1986.

Roach, M. *Another Name for Madness.* Houghton Mifflin. 1985.

Silverstone, B., & Hyman, H. *You and Your Aging Parent.* Pantheon. 1976.

Solotaroff, T. *Truth Comes In Blows.* W. W. Norton & Co. 1998.

Springer, D., & Brubaker, T. *Family Caregivers and Dependent Elderly.* Sage. 1984.

Szinovacz, M. *Women's Retirement.* Sage. 1982.

STATE AGENCIES ON AGING

ALABAMA
Commission on Aging
770 Washington Avenue, Suite 470
P.O. Box 301851
Montgomery, AL 36130
(334) 242-5743 or 1-800-243-5463

ALASKA
Division of Senior Services
3601 "C" Street, Suite 310
Anchorage, AK 99503
(907) 269-3680

ARIZONA
Aging & Adult Administration
Department of Economic Security
1789 West Jefferson Street, #950A
Phoenix, AZ 85007
(602) 542-4446

ARKANSAS
Division of Aging & Adult Services
7th and Main Streets
P.O. Box 1437/Slot 1412
Little Rock, AR 72201
(501) 682-2441

CALIFORNIA
Department of Aging
Health Insurance Counseling
    & Advocacy Branch
1600 K Street
Sacramento, CA 95814
(916) 322-5290

COLORADO
Aging & Adult Services
Department of Social Services
110 - 16th Street, Suite 200
Denver, CO 80203-5202
(303) 620-4147

CONNECTICUT
Elderly Services Division
Department of Social Services
25 Sigourney Street
Hartford, CT 06106-5033
(860) 424-5274 or 1-800-443-9946

DELAWARE
Division of Services for Aging &
    Adults with Physical Disabilities
1901 North DuPont Highway
2nd Floor Annex Administration
    Building
New Castle, DE 19720
(302) 577-4791 or 1-800-223-9074

DISTRICT OF COLUMBIA
Office on Aging
441 Fourth Street NW, 9th Floor
Washington, DC 20001
(202) 724-5622

FLORIDA
Department of Elder Affairs
4040 Esplanade Way
Building B - Suite 152
Tallahassee, FL 32399
(850) 414-2000

GEORGIA
Division of Aging Services
Department of Human Resources
2 Peachtree Street NE, 36th Floor
Atlanta, GA 30303
(404) 657-5258

HAWAII
Executive Office on Aging
250 South Hotel Street, Suite 109
Honolulu, HI 96813-2831
(808) 586-0100

IDAHO
Commission on Aging
700 West Jefferson, Room 108
P.O. Box 83720
Boise, ID 83720-0007
(208) 334-2423

ILLINOIS
Department on Aging
421 East Capitol Avenue
Springfield, IL 62701
(217) 785-3356

INDIANA
Bureau of Aging & In-Home
    Services
402 West Washington Street, E-431
Indianapolis, IN 46207-7083
(317) 232-7020

IOWA
Department of Elder Affairs
200 Tenth Street
Clemens Building, 3rd Floor
Des Moines, IA 50309-3609
(515) 281-5187

KANSAS
Department on Aging
New England Building
503 South Kansas
Topeka, KS 66603-3404
(913) 296-4986

KENTUCKY
Division of Aging Services
Cabinet for Human Resources
275 East Main Street, 6 West
Frankfort, KY 40621
(502) 564-6930

LOUISIANA
Governor's Office of Elderly
    Affairs
P.O. Box 80374
412 North 4th Street
Baton Rouge, LA 70802
(504) 342-7100

MAINE
Bureau of Elder and Adult Services
State House, Station 11
Augusta, ME 04333
(207) 624-5335

MARYLAND
Office on Aging
State Office Building, Room 1007
301 West Preston Street
Baltimore, MD 21201
(410) 767-1100 or 1-800-243-3425

MASSACHUSETTS
Executive Office of Elder Affairs
1 Ashburton Place, 5th Floor
Boston, MA 02108
(617) 727-7750

MICHIGAN
Office of Services to the Aging
P.O. Box 30676
Lansing, MI 48909-8176
(517) 373-8230

MINNESOTA
Board on Aging
444 Lafayette Road
St. Paul, MN 55155-3843
(612) 296-2770 or 1-800-882-6262

MISSISSIPPI
Division of Aging & Adult Services
750 North State Street
Jackson, MS 39202
(601) 359-4929

MISSOURI
Division of Aging
Department of Social Services
P.O. Box 1337
615 Howerton Court
Jefferson City, MO 65102-1337
(573) 751-3082

MONTANA
Division of Senior & Long-Term
  Care
Department of Public Health
  & Human Services
111 North Sanders Street
P.O. Box 4210
Helena, MT 59604
(406) 444-7781

NEBRASKA
Department on Aging
State Office Building
P.O. Box 95044
301 Centennial Mall South
Lincoln, NE 68509
(402) 471-2306

NEVADA
Division for Aging Services
Department of Human Resources
340 North 11th Street, Suite 203
Las Vegas, NV 89101
(702) 486-3545

NEW HAMPSHIRE
Division of Elderly & Adult
  Services
Department of Health & Human
  Services
115 Pleasant Street
Annex Building No. 1
Concord, NH 03301-3843
(603) 271-4680

NEW JERSEY
Division of Senior Affairs
Department of Health & Senior
  Services
P.O. Box 807
Trenton, NJ 08625-0807
(609) 588-3139

NEW MEXICO
State Agency on Aging
La Villa Rivera Building
228 East Palace Avenue
Ground Floor
Santa Fe, NM 87501
(505) 827-7640

NEW YORK
State Office for the Aging
Empire State Plaza, Building 2
Albany, NY 12223
(518) 474-4425 or 1-800-342-9871

NORTH CAROLINA
Division of Aging
693 Palmer Drive
Caller Box 29531
Raleigh, NC 27626-0531
(919) 733-3983

NORTH DAKOTA
Aging Services Division
Department of Human Services
600 South 2nd Street, Suite 1-C
Bismarck, ND 58504
(701) 328-8989 or 1-800-755-8521

OHIO
Department of Aging
50 West Broad Street, 9th Floor
Columbus, OH 43215-5928
(614) 466-5500

OKLAHOMA
Aging Services Division
Department of Human Services
312 North East 28th Street
Oklahoma City, OK 73125
(405) 521-2327

OREGON
Department of Human Resources
Senior & Disabled Services Division
500 Summer Street N.E., 2nd Floor
Salem, OR 97310-1015
(503) 945-5811 or 1-800-232-3020

PENNSYLVANIA
Department of Aging
555 Walnut Street, 5th Floor
Harrisburg, PA 17101-1919
(717) 783-1550

PUERTO RICO
Governor's Office of Elderly
  Affairs
P.O. Box 50063
Old San Juan Station
San Juan, PR 00902
(787) 721-5710

RHODE ISLAND
Department of Elderly Affairs
160 Pine Street
Providence, RI 02903-3708
(401) 222-2858

SOUTH CAROLINA
Office on Aging
Department of Health & Human
  Services
P.O. Box 8206
Columbia, SC 29202-8206
(803) 253-6177

SOUTH DAKOTA
Office of Adult Services & Aging
700 Governors Drive
Pierre, SD 57501
(605) 773-3656

TENNESSEE
Commission on Aging
Andrew Jackson Building
9th Floor
500 Deaderick Street
Nashville, TN 37243-0860
(615) 741-2056

TEXAS
Department on Aging
4900 North Lamar, 4th Floor
Austin, TX 78751-2316
(512) 424-6840

UTAH
Division of Aging & Adult Services
120 North 200 West
Salt Lake City, UT 84145-0500
(801) 538-3910

VERMONT
Department of Aging & Disabilities
Waterbury Complex
103 South Main Street
Waterbury, VT 05671-2301
(802) 241-2400

VIRGINIA
Department for the Aging
1600 Forest Avenue
Preston Building, Suite 102
Richmond, VA 23229
(804) 662-9333

WASHINGTON
Aging & Adult Services
  Administration
Department of Social & Health
  Services
P.O. Box 45050
Olympia, WA 98504-5050
(360) 586-8753

WEST VIRGINIA
Bureau of Senior Services
State Capitol Complex
Holly Grove – Building 10
1900 Kanawha Boulevard East
Charleston, WV 25305-0160
(304) 558-3317

WISCONSIN
Bureau of Aging & LTC Resources
217 South Hamilton Street
Suite 300
Madison, WI 53703
(608) 266-2536

WYOMING
Division on Aging
139 Hathaway Building
Cheyenne, WY 82002-0710
(307) 777-7986

SAMPLE LIVING WILL

To: My family physicians, my lawyer, and any medical facility in whose care I happen to be, any individual who may become responsible for my health affairs, and all others whom it may concern:

I, being of sound mind and over 18 years of age, hereby issue a directive which I intend to be legally binding, which shall become effective at some future time, only under the following circumstances:

When I become unable to make my own decisions or express my wishes, AND

(CHOOSE ALL THAT YOU WANT TO APPLY)

_____If I have a terminal illness and/or

_____If I am permanently unconscious; and/or

_____If extraordinary life support procedures or "heroic measures" would be medically futile; and/or

Under the following circumstances *(please specify, for example, dementia, severe neurological illness or other permanent disabling condition to which you want the directive to apply)*_____

_____

_____

_____

Then I direct that my dying not be unreasonably prolonged; AND

(CHOOSE ONE)

_____I wish to have COMFORT CARE ONLY, which is directed only toward relieving pain and suffering, regardless of the progress of my disease.

_____I want CONSERVATIVE CARE, which is usual treatment (such as antibiotics) but not extraordinary treatment (such as cardiopulmonary resuscitation, mechanical ventilation, kidney dialysis, etc.).

_____OPTIONAL: I wish to make additional directions (about life-support equipment or other matters) _____

_____

_____

_____

PLEASE NOTE: If, at some future time, you cannot make decisions for yourself, New York State law prohibits withholding artificial nutrition and hydration from you, unless you have already made your wishes known.

If I cannot eat or drink enough because of my irreversible medical conditions:

I DO   I DO NOT   *(CIRCLE ONE)*

want artificial nutrition (intravenous or tube feeding) and hydration (intravenous fluids).

In the absence of my ability to give directions regarding the aforementioned life-sustaining procedures, it is my intention that this direction shall be honored as the final expression of my legal right to refuse medical treatment and to accept the consequences of such refusal.

I understand the full importance of this directive, and I have signed it after thorough consideration of the nature and consequences of my refusal of such extraordinary life-support procedures, including their benefits and disadvantages. This directive is in accordance with my strong convictions and beliefs and is made freely without any inducement or coercion from any person or institution.

_____   _____
Signature   Date

I hereby certify that I am over 18 years of age and that I have witnessed the above declarant's signature.

_____   _____
Witness   Witness

_____   _____
Printed Witness Name   Printed Witness Name

_____   _____
Date   Date

SAMPLE HEALTH-CARE PROXY

I, _____ , hereby appoint the following
person as my health-care agent, to make any and all health-care
decisions for me except for any restrictions I have noted below.
This Proxy shall take effect when and if I become unable to
make my own health-care decisions.

_____   _____
Health-Care Agent Name   Area Code & Phone

_____
Address (Street, City, State, Postal code)

_____   _____
Alternate Health-Care   Area Code & Phone
Agent Name

_____
Address (Street, City, State, Postal code)

Optional instructions or limitations on the Health-Care Agent's
authority, if any: _____
_____
_____
_____

Unless I revoke it, this Proxy shall remain in effect indefinitely
(or until the date or condition stated hereafter if any):
_____
_____
_____

*PLEASE NOTE: If, at some future time, you cannot make
decisions for yourself, New York State law prohibits your Health-
Care Agent from making decisions about withholding artificial
nutrition and hydration from you, unless you have already made
your wishes known.*

If I cannot eat or drink enough because of my irreversible medical conditions:

I DO   I DO NOT   *(CIRCLE ONE)*

want artificial nutrition (intravenous or tube feeding) and hydration (intravenous fluids).

_____   _____
Signature   Date

I hereby certify that I am over 18 years of age, and that the person who signed this Proxy appeared to do so willingly and free from duress, and that he or she signed (or asked another to sign for him or her) this Proxy in my presence.

_____   _____
Witness   Witness

_____   _____
Printed Witness Name   Printed Witness Name

_____   _____
Date   Date

Readers:

Do you have an Eldercare story
that you would like to share?

If so, I would love to
hear from you.

We are planning a second edition
of this book and hope that your
story can be included.

Just send your story to:

Linda Meyer
403 South Wright Street
Champaign, IL 61820

Linda Meyer, Ph.D.

AUTHOR AND
CERTIFIED FAMILY THERAPIST

is available for seminars or talks on
the following topics:

- Eldercare
- Working With Adolescents
- Helping Children From
  Troubled Families To Recover

in addition to professional
services as a
Certified Family Therapist
or Mediator.

Linda can be reached at
(217) 367-8821
or by mail at
403 South Wright Street
Champaign, Illinois 61820

OTHER BOOKS AVAILABLE
FROM LINDA MEYER

ALL PROCEEDS FROM THE SALE OF THESE BOOKS GO TO THE KATELYN HUBBELL FUND. Katelyn is a 5-year-old girl with aplastic anemia scheduled to receive a bone-marrow transplant.

Interested persons can get to know Katy by visiting her website at **www.themiraclekids.com.**

Linda, please send me the following:

___ copies of *I See Myself Changing: Weekly Meditations and Recovery Journaling for Young Adults*   @ $12.95 _____

___ copies of *Recovery 101: A Meditation Journal for Young Adults and the Young At Heart*   @ $15.95 _____

___ copies of *I Can Look At Me: A Colorbook and Drawing Book on Recovery for Children 4-10*   @ $ 7.95 _____

Postage & handling for total order $ 3.50

TOTAL ORDER AMOUNT $ _____

Checks should be made payable to Emmanuel Memorial Episcopal Church, indicating "Katy's Fund" on the memo line. Please print your information on the lines below:

NAME _____

AREA CODE/PHONE NO. _____

ADDRESS _____

CITY/STATE/ZIP _____

Mail check & order form to:
Linda Meyer, 403 S. Wright St., Champaign IL 61820.

Thank you!

ℜecovery Communications, ℑnc.
BOOK PUBLISHING & AUTHOR PROMOTIONS
Post Office Box 19910 • Baltimore, Maryland 21211, USA

Now available through your local bookstore!

Jennifer J. Richardson, M.S.W. *Diary of Abuse/Diary of Healing.* A young girl's secret journal recording two decades of abuse, with detailed healing therapy sessions. A raw and extraordinary book that will inspire other abuse survivors with new hope. **Contact the author at (404) 373-1837.**

Toby Rice Drews. *Getting Them Sober, Volume One — You Can Help!* Hundreds of ideas for sobriety and recovery. The million-seller endorsed by Melody Beattie, Dr. Norman Vincent Peale, and "Dear Abby." **Contact the author at (410) 243-8352.**

Toby Rice Drews. *Getting Them Sober, Volume Four — Separation Decisions.* All about detachment, separation, and child custody issues for families of alcoholics. A "book of immense value," says Max Weisman, M.D., past president of the American Society of Addiction Medicine. **Contact the author at (410) 243-8352.**

Betsy Tice White. *Turning Your Teen Around: How A Couple Helped Their Troubled Son While Keeping Their Marriage Alive and Well.* A doctor family's successful personal battle against teen-age drug use, with powerfully helpful tips for parents in pain. Endorsed by John Palmer, former news anchor, NBC's TODAY Show. **Contact the author at (770) 590-7311.**

Betsy Tice White. *Mountain Folk/Mountain Food: Down-Home Wisdom, Plain Tales, and Recipe Secrets from Appalachia.* The joy of living as expressed in delightful vignettes and mouth-watering regional foods. Endorsed by the Discovery Channel's "Great Country Inns" and *Blue Ridge Country Magazine.* **Contact the author at (770) 590-7311.**

Linda Meyer, Ph.D. *I See Myself Changing: Weekly Meditations and Recovery Journaling for Young Adults.* A life-affirming book for adolescents and young adults, endorsed by Robert Bulkeley of The Gilman School. **Contact the author at (217) 367-8821.**

Mattie Carroll Mullins. *JUDY: The Murder of My Daughter, The Healing of My Family.* A Christian mother's inspiring story of how her family moved from unimaginable tragedy to forgiveness. **Contact the author at (423) 926-7827.**

Joseph C. Buccilli, Ph.D. *Wise Stuff About Relationships: Spiritual Reflections and Recovery Journal.* A gem of a book for anyone in recovery; "an empowering spiritual workout." Endorsed by the vice-president of the *Philadelphia Inquirer.* **Contact the author at (609) 629-4441.**

Stacie Hagan and Charlie Palmgren. *The Chicken Conspiracy: Breaking the Cycle of Personal Stress and Organizational Mediocrity.* A liberating message from corporate trainers about successful personal, organizational, and global change. **Contact the authors at (404) 297-9388.**

David E. Bergesen. *Murder Crosses the Equator: A Father Jack Carthier Mystery.* Volcanic tale of suspense in a Latin-American setting, starring a clever missionary-priest detective. **Contact the author at (520) 744-2631.**

John Pearson. *Eastern Shore Beckonings.* Marvelous trek back in time through charming villages and encounters with solid Chesapeake Bay folk. "Aches with affection" — The *Village Voice's* Washington correspondent. **Contact the author at (410) 315-7940.**

Jerry Zeller. *The Shaman and Other Almost-Tall Tales.* The enchantment of story-telling and grace-filled character sketches from an Episcopal archdeacon and former Emory University Dean. **Contact the author at (706) 692-5842.**

AND COMING SOON . . .

Jane Griz Jones. *From Grief To Gladness: Coming Back From Widowhood.* A Christian educator shares personal heartbreak and wisdom for reclaiming joy in life.